ONE ON ONE

The Best Women's Monologues for the Nineties

D0166983

Other titles from **THE APPLAUSE ACTING SERIES**

ACTING IN FILM (book & videocassette) Michael Caine

ACTING IN RESTORATION COMEDY Simon Callow

DIRECTING THE ACTION Charles Marowitz

MICHAEL CHEKHOV: ON THEATRE AND THE ART OF ACTING
(audiotapes) Mala Powers (ed.)

THE MONOLOGUE WORKSHOP Jack Poggi

ON SINGING ONSTAGE David Craig

RECYCLING SHAKESPEARE Charles Marowitz

SHAKESCENES: SHAKESPEARE FOR TWO John Russell Brown

SPEAK WITH DISTINCTION Edith Skinner

STANISLAVSKI REVEALED Sonia Moore

STANISLAVSKI TECHNIQUE: RUSSIA Mel Gordon

THE CRAFTSMEN OF DIONYSUS Jerome Rockwood

THE ACTOR AND THE TEXT Cicely Berry

**ONE ON ONE: THE BEST MEN'S MONOLOGUES FOR THE
NINETIES** Jack Temchin (ed.)

SHAKESPEARE'S PLAYS IN PERFORMANCE John Russell Brown

A PERFORMER PREPARES: A Guide to Song Preparation David Craig

The APPLAUSE ACTING SERIES

ONE ON ONE

The Best Women's Monologues for the Nineties

EDITED BY JACK TEMCHIN

APPLAUSE
NEW YORK • LONDON

From the APPLAUSE ACTING SERIES
An APPLAUSE original.
One on One: The Best Women's Monologues for the Nineties
Copyright © 1993 by Applause Theatre Books

An extension of this copyright notice, together with CAUTION and performance rights information, will be found in the "Play Sources and Acknowledgements" section at the end of the book.

Library of Congress Cataloging-in-Publication Data

One on one: the best women's monologues for the nineties / edited by
    Jack Temchin.
          p.   cm. — (The Applause acting series)
        ISBN 1-55783-152-1 (pbk.) : $7.95
        1. Monologues. 2. Acting. 3. Drama—20th century. I. Temchin,
    Jack. II. Series.
    PN2080.058   1993
    822'.04508—dc20   93-6790
                                               CIP

Applause Theatre Books
211 West 71 Street, New York, NY 10023
phone: 212-595-4735 fax: 212-721-2856

CONTENTS

"All the World's an Audition"

Everybody in the theater auditions. Even casting directors. The day I spoke to Meg Simon, whose office walls are festooned with the shows she's cast (*Amadeus*, *M. Butterfly*, and *Conversations with My Father* are a few), she was proudly telling friends that she had won the competition to cast *Angels in America*. The news was particularly sweet since other top casting agents were up for the job. Her entire career up to that moment had been her audition.

At about the same time, Jeff Ash, head of Grey Entertainment Advertising, was nervously waiting to hear if he was going to handle a big show from the West Coast. *He* had auditioned by presenting artwork and a proposed advertising campaign.

Everybody in theater faces his or her own audition. Yes, theater *producers*, too! Stanley Brechner, who runs the American Jewish Theater, before the first preview of every show, utters this prayer: "Please God, don't let it be a total and complete embarrassment." Everybody in the theater is subjected again and again to the rigors of being tested. You're not alone.

Yet there's no denying that you, the actor, face the most terrifying audition of all. It's just you and the listener. It's what your parents meant when they told you life is even harder than that final high school exam. It's a test of your guts and skill.

This introduction will not teach you how to do a job you probably already know how to do: act. Advice on "choosing the monologue," "preparing the monologue," and "presenting the monologue," are just fancy ways of telling you how to act. It's probably a good idea to be suspicious of the kind of acting advice you get from book editors anyway. Let me give you an example.

In 1961, I was fifteen and lucky enough to meet Richard Burton and watch him backstage several times in *Camelot*.

One of the highpoints of that show is a monologue by King Arthur that closes the first act. In it, Arthur realizes that his wife, Guenevere, and his best friend, Lancelot, are in love. But he decides to rise above his anger and act as a king, not a jealous husband. The subtext of this thrilling speech is Arthur's attainment of manhood, something he has been striving for since the beginning of the play.

The first time I saw Burton deliver it from backstage, I was surprised to see the entire cast watching from the wings. I asked someone if this happened a lot. "Every night," he assured me. I knew I was watching the ultimate tribute an actor can receive: the admiration of his peers from the wings.

Now, in the acting-advice business, *preparation* is a sacred prescription. Any teaching guru who would suggest otherwise would be a) labeled a heretic and/or b) out of a job! But every night Burton would disdain the profound preparation rituals we all hear so much about. Instead, Richard Burton prepared for his monologue by sipping a cocktail and talking to friends he invited to come by—people like Lauren Bacall and Jason Robards. Until, on cue, his dresser and friend, Bob Wilson, signaled, "It's time." Burton would calmly take a final sip, put down his drink, put on his cape, nod good-bye to us, walk out of his dressing room, pick up his sword, and step on stage. And deliver! So much for preparation! Afterwards, Burton would immediately return to his dressing room and pick his drink back up, perfectly relaxed. As Burton's own career will attest, martinis may not be the best prescription either. Whatever works for you, I'm not going to prescribe it for you here.

I am going to offer you many monologues to work on.

Both Meg Simon and Randy Carrig, the casting director of the Manhattan Theatre Club, emphasize that the choice of monologue is the single most important clue they have about you as an actor. Simon says it's like introducing yourself at a party. She forms an impression of your tastes and education through the material you choose to perform. While she stresses that she prefers "light audition pieces (suffering by request only)," she really enjoys actors who are part of "new theater...in touch with emerging playwrights." She likes risk-takers.

Carrig goes further about material, saying he often asks who wrote the particular play the monologue is from and what the actor thinks about it. If the actor doesn't know who wrote it (shockingly, that happens a lot) or can't express his thoughts about it, he suspects the actor isn't deeply conscientious or commited to his or her work. After all, if you haven't taken the interest to research your own piece, it doesn't say much for how deeply you'll explore a play somebody else casts you in. It leaves the listener with the distinct impression of a casual superficiality towards the work—not the trait you want to be remembered for.

Which is where this book comes in. In the hope that you'll want to read the original play from which a *One on One* mononlogue you like was extracted, I've offered you some background about each of the plays in question.

If you take casting directors Simon and Carrig seriously, you'll eventually have to figure out what engages *you* about the entire play you've chosen. They'll want to know what's going through your mind.

You'll notice another thing: there are some pieces here that probably don't fit you—you're probably hovering in your twenties or thirties and auditioning for parts of that age. I've included a few pieces for actors as old as seventy (Pinter's *Party Time,* in the female version of *One on One*), Irish (*Dances at Lughnasa*), and even hermaphrodites. The reason is that I enjoy these monologues as pieces of writing. They may not be all that useful to you as audition pieces, but they may just make your life a little fuller, a little better for having just read them. Or you might just learn them anyway to sharpen certain skills of acting and speaking. But Meg Simon warns that if you choose to do *Dances at Lughnasa,* say, make sure you do the Irish accent; otherwise she'll assume you can't.

What's the piece for actors who are hermaphrodites? *Red Scare on Sunset* by Charles Busch in which Busch himself played the part of Mary Dale, who is very much a lady. See where you fit into that one! (I decided to put it into the *female* version of the book.)

I've included Harold Pinter's *Party Time* for its excellence, but the *female* monologue from it is in for another reason as well. It's spoken by a character who is seventy years old, and I hope some young actresses out there will give it a try. I'm tired of actors playing age by putting on tons of makeup and latex. That happens in the movies, of course. But you can actually "act" aging in the theater. The physical distance of your audience from you (and the aesthetic one, too) allows you to work without latex. What you need is practice. Pinter's play gives you ample opportunity.

Actually, what "fits" you as an actor is a tricky proposition. Conventional wisdom tells you to choose a monologue that suits you: if you're fat, don't play a gaunt; if you're a guy, don't play a doll; if you're young, don't play old, etc. Well, in 1972, I produced a play in a workshop at Lincoln Center called *Kool-Aid*. It was made up of two one-acts. One was set in a drug addict's apartment that served as a shooting gallery. Various addicts made their appearance and their speeches. One of these characters was a guy named Fat, who was just that.

I thought a friend of mine who had performed in an off-Broadway show was perfect for the role. When I offered it to him, he was offended because, "The only reason you want me for this role is that I'm fat." Actually, I thought of him for the part because he was funny and touching and a very good actor. When he turned me down, I suggested to the director an unknown actor I had seen in a movie, *Hi Mom!* That actor was funny and thin. But he never blinked when we asked him to audition.

His name was Robert DeNiro.

He read for the part and was very thin and very funny and he got the job.

Another play I produced, *El Grande de Coca-Cola*, needed a replacement actor, who at one point in the play would comically portray Tolouse Lautrec. The tall Jeff Goldblum auditioned. A lot of the humor in that bit now came from the sight of Jeff playing the part on his knees—especially since Jeff on his knees is still about the same height as any normal person on his feet. He got laughs, not because he *couldn't* play Lautrec, but because he successfully "acted" small, giving the audience enough details of this dwarfish character that they could see beyond the lanky form on the stage. He, too, got the part he was after.

Most of the monologues in this book have been chosen with a generalized "you" in mind—the "you" that can be summed up by the age in parentheses on the contents page and the character descriptions accompanying the monologues. What's people like Meg Simon and Randy Carrig are looking for in your audition is the *real* you, the individual spirit who can give a character life beyond written specifications in the script.

Here's how Ron Silver showed me *his* individuality. *El Grande de Coca-Cola* had become a big hit, in spite of the fact that it was mostly in Spanish (with some French and Italian and German, no English). We needed a replacement for the lead. The main requirement was that the actor be fluent in Spanish. Which meant that three quarters of those whom I interviewed tried to fake it with their year or two of high school Spanish.

The reason I was casting the replacement was that I had had a year or two of high school Spanish myself and could spot a fellow phoney a mile away.

After seeing two hundred actors, I decided the auditions were over and closed the door. A few minutes later, there was a terrible knocking. And this voice started to demand entry in a Spanish I couldn't understand. So, I figured he was a really bad faker and was determined to keep him out. Until he brayed in perfect English: "If I don't get this job, I'll have to go to _____."

He named a summer theater known as the Dachau of summer theaters, so abusive was it of its apprentices and non-Equity personnel.

Now, this shameless attempt at manipulation betrayed a real desperation on the actor's part. Something a lot of TV commercials and monologue books tell you is wrong to show—it's another of those sacred rules. But in this case, the individual who broke that rule succeeded in catching my attention—when I was supposed to have my mind on language skills—because I had been an apprentice at Dachau Summer Theater years before and knew exactly what the guy meant.

I opened the door and there stood Ron Silver. After several auditions (all in Spanish, which it turns out Ron can speak fluently) and a bizarre improvisation (in which Ron vividly performed a monologue about being born without a head, in Spanish), he got the part.

Another rule-breaker who managed to draw attention to himself was a friend of mine who one day decided to break the rule about dressing well for auditions. He had always done so, but he never got cast. One casting director used to pitch him into a vicious cycle of elation and dejection by repeatedly calling him in—and each time dismissing him by saying: "Sorry, this time it wasn't meant to be, but how glad I am that we finally had a chance to meet." As if she hadn't seen him fifteen times before!

My friend shrewdly figured out he wasn't making much of an impression. So, the next time he got the call, he went into the men's room before the interview and he doused himself with water until he looked like Gene Kelley in *Singin' in the Rain*. He ruined a good suit, too. But when he walked in the lady was dumbstruck. He didn't get that part, but a few days later she remembered him and called him about another part. And that was the start of a career that has gotten him parts in movies like *Wired*, *Big Business*, and *Barfly* and a home in Santa Barbara—which he leaves to take parts when he feels like it.

Finally, you'll notice that the title of this book is a basketball term. Basketball has its rules. But, as I have urged you to be skeptical about all the rules that editors prescribe, let me tell you this story about someone who broke what I have earlier referred to as a *very* important rule.

A famous actress asked me to read a movie script she had been given. She was being offered a lot of money. She watched me read it, gauged my reaction, and then asked whether her character was credibly written. When I said yes, she asked me to explain why. As we talked it over, I realized *she hadn't read the script!*

"Oh, I just read my part!" she admitted cheerfully.

After I insisted that she read the whole script, she met with the director, who disagreed with her feelings about everything in it. Now, she was upset and wondering whether she should have taken the part in the first place. But coincidentally the director was fired and the new one rewrote the entire script. The actress was brilliant in the movie and ran away with the reviews. And she probably never read the new script!

So what do I know?

Yes, basketball has rules. Monologue books? Forget it!

—Jack Temchin

15

•Note: Brackets [   ] indicate that the speech is interrupted by another character in the original play. Most of these lines are well worth reading and thinking about as they will offer clues to the questions and issues which the main character is trying to answer.

•Note: If a monologue is too long for your audition or class, you may wish to judiciously cut the speech down to suit your purposes. While thinking about what can be cut from a speech, you'll also discover what's most important to the character and the dramatic moment. Whenever you do offer a cut version of any speech, you owe it to your audience to tell them so.

THE AMERICAN PLAN by Richard Greenberg

EVA ADLER, a wealthy German Jew in her sixties, speaks with a lush accent and a sharp tongue. She has reduced her daughter, Lili, to a state of perpetual obedience in all matters. Her overbearing manner is clear in the following breakfast conversation with Lili.

SCENE: A table outside the Adlers' summer home in the Catskills.

TIME: Early 1960's.

EVA: ...And, then, we all repaired to the club where the most mystifying entertainer held forth...if only I could remember his name!... He was...how do you say it...*crossed-eyed*, with vast jowls and this idiotic, juvenile voice, and, of course, his language was quite improper, and what he said was simply nonsense, yet those around me *howled*, as though these were the pearls of Oscar Wilde being thrown before them. Unutterably fascinating! I wanted you to be there, Lili, to assure me I had not *lost* my mind. Everyone asked after you at dinner—aren't you hungry, why aren't you eating? Olivia has prepared for us a lovely porridge. That's good. At any rate, I had a pencil with me, my little gold pencil, and I recorded my impressions of the event on a cocktail napkin, lest I forget them. What an extraordinary evening. Yet, not at all...untypical...for the region. Ve-e-e-ry strange. That darling Mindy Kahkstein was there. A *m-o-ost* peculiar girl. One of those American girls who can't seem to get used to their bosoms. To show or not to show. To slump or stand erect. You feel these are her sole concerns. She asked after you. And, of course, I spent time with Libby Kahkstein—a woman who is *très cher*, but not, I think, intellectually robust. And, once again, she disgraced herself at table. Why, when I tell you what she ate, and in what quantities! The *salad*— served at the beginning—barbaric, anyway, but Libby tore into it like a savage woman. And the Russian dressing—not just a dollop, either,

17

but *gobules*—Gobules?...—*Globules.* Then the consomme, then the derma, smothered in gravy and onions, then the filet mignon—a steak the size and shape of a jackboot also smothered in gravy. With a vast baked potato, into which Libby Kahkstein scooped not merely sour cream and chives, but five pats of butter. *Plus* asparagus with hollandaise. *Plus,* infinite numbers of buttered rolls, with seeds popping everywhere. *Plus* sherbet between courses. *Plus,* barrels of cream soda. *Plus,* coffee with heavy cream and parfait. Then—*then*—after the meal was over, and there was a little desultory dancing—out came this enormous Viennese Table. And Libby Kahkstein—using every ounce of energy available to her simply to transport her laden bulk—helped herself not *once*, not *twice*, but *three* times. To Napoleon, Sacher Torte, and a large plate of little cookies. *Incroyable!* But my darling, why aren't you eating your breakfast?

ANTIGONE IN NEW YORK by Janusz Glowacki

Homeless people in lower New York, trying to retrieve the body of their friend Paulie and give him a decent burial. Here, ANITA, Puerto Rican, thirty-five, has just been told that her lover, Paulie, has died. The night before, she had given him a cashmere sweater from a church charity.

SCENE: Tompkins Square Park, New York City.

TIME: The present.

ANITA: Can I ask you just one thing? Are you sure he's dead? Because so many things could happen around here. I mean, he could have just passed out or something or fallen asleep under something where no one could see him. He could have gotten drunk. Are you absolutely sure? Because sometimes people get confused and think they see one thing but really it's something else. You have to be one hundred percent sure. [SASHA: I'm telling you that's what the police said.] The Indian told me the ambulance took him too but I don't trust him. He's always lying. You know what I mean? [SASHA: If the ambulance took him it means he's dead.] *(weeping into her hands)* I knew it. It was that cashmere sweater. I let it get to me. I knew it was

18

bad luck but I took it anyway. They were giving it away and I just couldn't leave it there. This sweater belonged to some unhappy person. Happy people don't wear cashmere sweaters but unhappy people, they are either too cold or too hot and instead of going to the doctor they buy a cashmere sweater and when they put it on they start sweating right away and then their sweat goes into the cashmere and their bad luck sticks to it. You can wash it. You can even dry clean it but it won't do any good. The bad luck stays in the sweater no matter what you do. *(she drinks the cold coffee and throws the empty cup into the trash basket)* If you have to wear a cashmere sweater it's best to get one with shoulder pads in it because that's where the bad luck collects. Then you can just pull out the pads and throw them away. That helps. I did that right away but it just wasn't enough. I felt it when I got it. But now it's too late. *(weeps more, and opens her coat to show him)* See? [SASHA: What?] This is acryllic. And acryllic is no problem. You just take it off and shake it a couple of times *(she demonstrates)* and the bad luck disappears. *(praying again)* What am I going to do?

APPROXIMATING MOTHER by Kathleen Tolan

We see the trauma of adoption both from the point of view of the birth mother and the woman who adopts the child.

JEN, sixteen, tells the counselor of her decision not to abort her unborn child. She's giving it up for adoption after all.

SCENE: The office of a counselor for unwed mothers in New York City.

TIME: The present.

(JEN and SYLVIA sit in Sylvia's office. Jen is about six months pregnant.)

JEN: I didn't use anything. And I thought about it a lot while we were doing it, thought I should say something but I guess I felt shy so I kept putting it off. And then I thought, well, he won't go all the way without asking if I'm on the pill or getting some rubbers or something. And then he was inside me and I kept putting it off and didn't want to interrupt and then he came inside me and I thought, "shit." But then I thought, well, I'm not so regular anyway, so who knows when I'm going to be ovulating. Think of all the times I *haven't* done it this month. The odds are really good I was ovulating one of those times. So when my period was late, I thought, "Shit—" but then, well, it's been late before and I just tried not to think about it. And I started feeling really bloated and my breasts started getting really tender and big but I really just tried not to think about it. Finally I couldn't zip my jeans and I faced the fact I had to do something so I called my girlfriend Brena and she helped me find a clinic and we went to the doctor and he said I was pregnant and I said I wanted an abortion and he said I had to have permission from my parents and I said I didn't want to tell them and he told me I should go to this social worker woman— Um. Her name was Mrs. Nelson. Um. I don't know. He just gave me her number. And said she'd help me and wouldn't tell my parents so I went to her and she told me I would regret it if I had an abortion and I said I regretted this whole thing but that's what I wanted to do and I didn't want to have a baby, I wanted to finish high school and stuff and she said if I wasn't ready to be a mother there were many wonderful couples who would love a baby and I said, well that's fine but I don't want to do that so she said I needed to have permission from my parents and then I should come back to her and she'd help me but I should think about how I'd feel if my parents had decided not to have me and I said, "huh?" And she said she knew this must be a very scary and confusing time for me and I should know she was my friend and I said I didn't think so and then she got really nasty because she knew I could see right through her and she started screeching, "Go ahead, kill the baby. Kill the baby. See how it makes you feel." And some day I'd wish I had a baby, wouldn't I and I said I don't know what you're talking about, let me out of here and went home and went up to my room and was just shaking and crying and I told my mom I had the flu and just stayed up there for a couple of days and finally I told my mom I was pregnant. And then everybody completely freaked out and here I am.

APPROXIMATING MOTHER by Kathleen Tolan

We see the trauma of adoption both from the point of view of the birth mother and the woman who adopts the child.

FRAN, forty, unable to find the perfect mate, decides to adopt a child. She uses her child adoption attorney as a sounding board for her own feelings which led to this momentous decision.

SCENE: A lawyer's office.

TIME: The present.

FRAN: I haven't wanted, in my life, to compromise. I mean, when it really mattered to me—but, you know, a lot of my friends, because they wanted to go somewhere, get somewhere, you know, have a certain amount of success, um, are doing things, representing things or, um, philosophies, ideas, they never would have...And there's been, often, the question of how to support the children—Yes. Yes. And the question, too, "Am I really willing, at age forty, to live in quite the austerity I embraced in my twenties." Yes. And as a woman, you know, you hold out for as long as you can for the man who will really—I mean, *really* think of you as a, like, actual person, autonomous, with *really* as much of a right to a whole life. I mean, I think there are men who are now able to think of a woman as separate but equal as a colleague but not as a wife. Obviously there are exceptions and I haven't read a study or anything but it is my feeling. Anyway—sorry—I am getting to the—this is leading somewhere. I just never felt I *really* would be able to, you know, not be "the wife," however "modern" he might seem. With every—not that there were so many—serious relationship, I felt, however unconsciously, that I should be serving him. Or that—that I couldn't—couldn't *really* have my own thoughts. My own private thoughts. Anyway, not pretending to be, you know, a moral arbiter, just trying to retain my integrity. Certainly I'm sophisticated enough to know one's own neuroses are always tied up in—in fact, often *inform*, if not *determine*, one's philosophy, one's actions. Um. (*Pause*) Anyway, with all of this, finally feeling very, sort of, lonely and, you know, "Is this it?" And then beginning to think about a baby. Wanting that, the feeling, the sensuality—the basicness of, you know, the tasks. And the clarity of one's priorities, one's own reason for, you know, carrying on. And of course, they're so sweet. And I imagine I would feel more...connected to, you know, life, to the cycle, to the world, to humanity. And, I guess, it seems *manageable*. I mean, so much in the world seems so overwhelming, so impossible. This would be a life I might actually have some effect on. Not that I would—I mean, I'd try to honor her or him, to help and guide but not to impose my own...And, I guess, to feel connected to the—the awe—to the mystery—I don't mean the mystery of birth and life, though, of course, but, I see it with my friends, that the most basic, most boring—to the outsider—achievements of their young children are absolutely thrilling. It's as if they themselves are children again, are experiencing the miracle of—of how the world works and what it is to be alive. And, of course the problems that arise can be quite daunting, but, again, the scale seems...manageable.

THE ART OF SUCCESS by Nick Dear

We know William Hogarth perfected the art of selling prints of both lowlife and public personalities. And Nick Dear adds that he sold his soul, in the process. The play uses people and events of the past to talk about timeless issues like censorship, artistic license, and an artist's conscience when the state opposes him.

Hogarth is sketching SARAH, a woman in her twenties about to die by hanging. She sits in front of him, thoroughly at ease and unselfconscious. Dirty and coarse, and without illusions, Sarah tells him how she wants to be remembered.

SCENE: A London prison cell.

TIME: The 1730's.

SARAH *(smiles)*: ...As long as people see that I am bad. I want to be bad. That's how I want to be remembered. As an insult. A spit in the face. Do me like that. *(WILLIAM nods.)* I could kill you for the food, I s'pose...But I can't be bothered. Not after I just had a wash. *(They both resume their seats.)* [WILLIAM: Christ what a day. *(He draws.)*] A blunt razor I used to kill the old women. The widow's memento of her long-dead man. I was that ravenous, I had ceased to think, and that felt good, you can think too much when you're starving. I knew that my mistress's treasure was under her cot. So I bled the bitch and her bedmate while they slept. *(Laughs.)* Two stuck pigs in their petticoats. The rage, the urge to eat crept over me, and I succumbed. The peacefulest moment I ever have known...that second I abandoned trying to be good. You throw off the wretched, useless rags you've gone cold in all your life—the common sense, the reason—throw it to the wind and go naked, raw, free suddenly...Then Mary, the maid, with who I shared the attic, appeared on the stair, so I had to kill her too, aren't you done yet? [*WILLIAM is sitting with his chalk held in mid-air. Then he scrawls on the bottom of the paper, and is finished.* WILLIAM *(quiet)*: The two old women, yes, I kind of understand, I read that they mistreated you...but the maid? Why the maid? Why on earth?] Shrieked at the blood, soppy cow. I knew that if I was committing the perfect. crime I could scarce afford to leave a witness. [WILLIAM: ...Why'd you get caught then?] Ah. Don't know. I can't explain things. Not in words. I never even managed to sell the damn silver. So hunger follows me down to the lime-pit.

THE ART OF SUCCESS by Nick Dear

We know William Hogarth perfected the art of selling prints of both lowlife and public personalities. And Nick Dear adds that he sold his soul, in the process. The play uses people and events of the past to talk about timeless issues like censorship, artistic license, and an artist's conscience when the state opposes him.

Hogarth is constantly aroused by JANE, his twenty-something wife. He is now proposing that they make love in public. She refuses and goes home. Alone and preparing for bed, she has second and third thoughts.

SCENE: The HOGARTHS' house. A large bed. Moonlight coming through a window. Flickering shadows from candles in corners. Jane is in her nightclothes, brushing her hair.

TIME: The 1730's.

JANE: Listen, my hair crackles with desire. Why don't you come home? William? I would do now what you wanted in the park. I just must be private, it is my nature. Under my sheets I will do anything, nothing's too dirty for my little man. He will come a million times. His heart will burst from coming.

(She looks out of the window.)

This is all assuming he gets home within the next five minutes, because otherwise, forget it, I'm not that devoted to the idea.

(She gets into bed and blows out her candle.)

His hands! I can't rid my thoughts of his hands. Stubby fingers exploring the bones in my back, grimy nails that rasp on silk, slipping, sliding, tumbling down my grassy slopes…We lie for hours, twined like rope, like vines, all licks and dribbles, tooth on grape, inner thigh—

(Silent and unseen, Sarah enters, and listens.)

—on inner thigh, he calls it the Line of Beauty, perpetual spiral of perfect art—we lose our limbs, begin to blend—we become snakes, we slither together—our flicking tongues—oh William—

THE ART OF SUCCESS by Nick Dear

MRS. NEEDHAM, a madame of street girls, has been clapped in the pillories. She bemoans her fate. Behind her, eighteenth-century artist William Hogarth, stripped naked by an angry prostitute he has neglected to pay, comes upon Needham and takes her clothes. She cannot see her abuser.

SCENE: London. A pillory at night.

TIME: The 1730's.

NEEDHAM: God is good. *(Pause.)* God is just. *(Pause.)* He is, he is! Prostitution is a wicked trade, I knew he wouldn't like it. But this

24

sinner will hang on her cross, O merciful Father, until she hears your voice call down from heaven in forgiveness, Needham, the Bawd, you have suffered enough, pucker your lips on the soles of my feet, we shall enter Jerusalem together. I wish to announce my retirement from business. I have some capital, Lord, not as much as I'd hoped for given my talents—oh, I was a goer in my time, I could take ten bob with my legs together—but that was when I freelanced. Once you become an employer your overheads hit the roof...And the paperwork!

(Behind her, WILLIAM comes on out of the dark. He still wears only sheet and wig. He creeps on furtively, shaking with cold.)

But if I survive the night, Christ Jesus, I will give my life and my savings to your mission on earth. Let me be your handmaiden, let me be your scourge in the city of sin. For I know the guilty. I can name names. You will see some blushing faces I promise you!— Who's there?

(WILLIAM's behind her. She can't turn round.)

Who is it? Come where I can see you. I smell you! You reek of gin.

(WILLIAM just stands there.)

Don't hurt me, don't harm me, I haven't done anything awful, but a mob of screaming puritans got hold of me tonight, priests and thin women, I don't mind, allow them their outrage, there was a wave of morality burst upon us after Mr Walpole's constables had raided that theatre. And they dragged me to the Justice and he slammed me in the stocks! And then the apprentice boys pushed stones in their rotten tomatoes, and pelted me half to death! If you would wipe my face...? Be kind to me...? I'm cut in a thousand places...by the fruit of the self-righteous...

(WILLIAM puts a hand on her.)

Oh! Mister! Your hand on my rump...I have the hindquarters of a horse, haven't I? I once heard of a gentleman who said England was a paradise for women, and hell for horses. Well he can take me out for a canter any old time. Little dig in the flanks and I'm off mate. Oh, don't abuse me, don't, I feel so vulnerable, I'm dripping blood and egg-yolk, I can see it in on the ground, like a little kiddie's painting of the sun.

(WILLIAM, from behind, pulls off the woman's skirt and puts it round himself.)

Don't please! I'm dry! I'll scrape! A whore can be raped, you know, just as a bankrupt can be swindled. Lord Jesus protect me...

(WILLIAM pulls off her blouse and puts that on.)

Do I know you? Is that it? Are you someone I have had? Some complainer out of all the happy thousands, bent on getting it for nothing? Will you speak to me you pervert!

(WILLIAM tries on her shoes. They fit.)

I will die of freezing...I'll be gone by dawn...But God will punish you. God will burn your lecher's eyes out. He will tear at your heart with his fingernails. God's fingernails, matey, think of that! God's rasping scratching omnipresent nails!

(WILLIAM, now dressed, drapes the sheet over the woman's head, and leaves.)

Wanker! Pass by on the other side, then! Go on! Pass by! I can hear you shuffling away...Devil!

(He is gone. Pause. Slowly her head droops.)

Lord have mercy on me. Christ have mercy on me. Lord have mercy on me. Christ have mercy on me.

BEAU JEST by James Sherman

Much to her parents' consternation, SARAH GOLDMAN, a Jewish woman in her twenties, has been seeing a Christian man named Chris. Thinking she's very clever, Sarah has told her parents she's dumped him for a proper Jewish guy, but, in fact, she's still seeing Chris on the sly. Of course, the plot thickens when her parents want to meet the new Jewish boyfriend. Sarah has hired an escort to impersonate the Jewish boyfriend for a big dinner with her folks. She fills him in as she sets the table.

SCENE: A one bedroom apartment around Lincoln Park in Chicago.

TIME: The present.

SARAH: The whole thing is so stupid. But my parents...Well, you know...They're my parents. My dad was sick last year. My mother's been so tense. I just can't give them any grief right now. The worst of it was after I told them I'd stopped seeing Chris. They assumed I wasn't seeing anybody. So my mother kept trying to fix me

26

up with sons of friends and relatives and I don't know—strangers she'd meet on the street. I don't know *where* she found these guys. But my mother is determined to make me happy. Whether I like it or not. One time, I went to their house for dinner and she had clipped personal ads out of a magazine for me. Can you imagine? Looking down at your dinner plate and seeing brisket on one side and "S.W.M., mid-thirties, Jewish" on the other? [BOB *(Grimacing.)*: Ooh.] Really, I mean, I know she means well, but…So, anyway, just so they'd feel better a few months ago, I told them I'd started seeing someone. I just *invented* a boyfriend. [BOB: Oh. And that's…*(He points to himself.)*] Right. [BOB: Wow.] Well, my mother's been driving me crazy with "When are we going to meet him?" "When are we going to meet him?" I just couldn't put it off anymore. *(She places two Sabbath candlesticks on the table.)* She'll probably want to light candles. I thought about asking one of my friends to be my stand-in beau for the evening, but, frankly, I'm too embarrassed by the whole thing for anybody I know to know about it. So I called your agency. *(She looks at him.)* You must think this is extremely weird.

[BOB. Well, I must admit, I expected you to be a little old lady who needed a dinner companion…But this would have been my second guess.]

(She remembers what has to be done.) Oh, God. Listen. Pay attention. My father's name is Abe. He owns a chain of dry cleaning stores. My mother's name is Miriam. But I think you should call them Mr. and Mrs. Goldman. They live in Skokie on Kildare just off Dempster. And my brother'll be here, too. His name is Joel. He's a psychologist. He's divorced. He has two children. You and I have been dating since January. We met at the wedding of my best friend, Marilyn Dintenfass. You think you can remember that?

[BOB: Yeah, I guess…Only…Wow.]

What?

[BOB: Well, no, I guess I can handle it. Uh…See, all I heard was "You're going out with a Miss Sarah Goldman. You're going to dinner. Wear a suit."]

I'm sorry. I know this is crazy. It was all in kind of a rush. What do they say? "Desperation is the mother of invention?"

THE BELLEVUE OF THE WEST SIDE by Leonard Melfi

Twenty-five people caught up in the bustle of the Port Authority Bus Terminal all reach for one another rather than take from one another.

MISSY O'MESSY, a lovely eighteen year old, has just arrived via Greyhound from the Midwest in search of a career and a man—not necessarily in that order. She has more or less run away from home with enough money to last her about a week. She knows absolutely no one in the Big Apple.

SCENE: Port Authority Bus Terminal, New York City.

TIME: The present.

MISSY: I came to New York for a career. But I really just want to be in love. And then, of course, I want to be married. I want a husband forever, and I want our children. I never thought I'd be talking this way...but I met this guy yesterday, and well, he just really did it to me...he did it for me...what a guy...only I don't know where he is right now...if I did know, well, I'd be with him in a second: I wouldn't let him out of my sight...I'd do anything for him...and I don't even know him...and yet: I feel as if I do...God: I haven't felt this way since my first mad, wild crush when I was fourteen...that was four years ago...my parents used to think I was really strange because I fell for this guy who was eighteen who was on the football team and who also wrote poetry and played the piano, and I loved him because he played jazz, better jazz than this kind of jazz that's playing right now...and it was really strange because none of us kids knew about jazz...he was the only one who did in the whole high school, in the whole town, probably...it made him very special to me...and then one day it was all over...yes, all over for me, because it was all over for him, too, and I really mean ALL OVER for him!...because do you know what he went and did?!...he went and killed himself...he hung himself in the attic of his house...because he had cancer, and they were going to have to amputate his whole right arm.

(MISSY begins to cry.)
Please forgive me, Veronica. I'm sorry.

He played the piano, see?...he played football, see?...he wrote poetry, see?...he had the most beautiful handwriting you ever saw...his hand-written poems were works of art in themselves...you wanted to frame them, and the poems were awesome, believe me, Veronica. *(A pause.)* I was fourteen and he was eighteen. He never really knew how I felt about him. I guess it's better that he didn't. I didn't leave our house for three months after he was dead. And then yesterday I came here to New York. Alone. *(A pause.)* And then I met this guy. Only for a few minutes. But he looked just like Guy...that was his name: Guy...who killed himself...and this guy yesterday...not only did he look like Guy, but he acted and sounded like him, too: trying to be tough and naughty, but a real live heart-warming pussycat in the end. *(A pause.)* I think I'd better go now.

THE BELLEVUE OF THE WEST SIDE by Leonard Melfi

Twenty-five people caught up in the bustle of the Port Authority Bus Terminal all reach for one another rather than take from one another.

REBECCA VIRGIN, a thirty-year-old, sexy, sleazy 8th Avenue hooker, is especially popular with her customers for serving soup before and after sex. She doesn't just hook for the money—she truly enjoys her job. When it becomes tiring, though, she takes refuge in the bus terminal.

SCENE: Port Authority Bus Terminal, New York City.

TIME: The present.

REBECCA: I need some strong shit in my system, Bluebird Honey, and I need it real fast. I'm gettin' outa this business. After the first of the year, right after Christmas, in fact, then I'm sayin' good-bye. I'm tired. Some guy, just a little while ago, he brings his own condoms with him. Well, that's all right, but the ones he brings, he must have had them since the Civil War, or at least Pearl Harbor. Moths flew out of them, I swear to God Almighty! Moths flying out of condoms! What next?! Well, let me tell you: I'm not about to hang around and find out. This other guy, he likes to kiss a lot, too. You get them every so often. They want their money's worth. But this one?! He's got herpes on his lips. I tell him to lay off. He ain't kissing me no way on my lips. He ain't kissing me anywhere. But then he takes out a wad of bills. Big bills. The man is sick. He could get a real expensive thing and not have to worry about any disease or anything. But no, he's sick, and so he comes to my type...with his big fat wad of big bills. My eyes go bananas. I give in. I let him kiss my feet, my toes mainly, but I kept my stockings on. I made a nice little fortune from him.

THE BIG FUNK by John Patrick Shanley

Here, JILL, a woman in her twenties, introduces herself:

SCENE: The East Village, New York City.

TIME: The present.

JILL: Hello. Good evening. Whatever. My name is Jill. I am speaking to you directly from my subconscious mind. I do this to save time. I am a destructive person. I am not the hero of this play. I am not the hero of any play I could be in. Except a play I wrote. And even in my own play I wouldn't be the hero. It would be a tragedy of course. But it wouldn't be my tragedy. It would be the tragedy of existence. And it would be a bad play. Because it would be senseless. Because whatever had gone wrong with the world would've gone wrong before the play even started. It would just be a whole bunch of victims. And I would just be one of them. It would just be a mess of senseless pain. I wouldn't want to see this play, much less be in it. In fact, if I wrote this play I'm describing, and it was performed, and afterwards someone asked: Who wrote this play? I would just look around to see who raised her hand. This is because I am a coward. Which is the root of my problem. So I am not in a play of my own. And I am not the hero. And this is not a tragedy. And this is where I would rather be. In a play where I will fail to prevail. I want to be stopped. I cannot stop myself. I am not easy to stop. And I can do a lot of harm before I'm knocked down. I do have a noose around my own neck. But if I pull up on the rope, I will not die. I am condemned. I carry around my means of execution. But it's not for me to do the job. This is what makes people like me a real bummer. Somebody, for the sake of everybody, has to squash me and blot up my remains. God put me on earth. I am a villain. I have a job to do. I am going to do it.

BOLD GIRLS by Rona Munro

Several Irish women in Belfast struggle to keep their families intact and their hopes alive in the grime and fear of a Catholic-Protestant war.

MARIE, thirty-four, Catholic, mother of young Michael, Jr., now dead at the hands of the British, remembers, for her friends Cassie and Deidre, her wedding day.

SCENE: MARIE's house in Belfast, Ireland.

TIME: The present.

It is irons and ironing boards and piles of clothes waiting to be smoothed, socks and pegs and damp sheets waiting for a break in the Belfast drizzle for the line, it's toys in pieces and toys that are just cardboard boxes and toys that are new and gleaming and flashing with lights and have swallowed up the year's savings. It's pots and pans and steam and the kettle always hot for tea, it's furniture that's bald with age and a hearth in front of the coal fire that's gleaming clean.

MARIE: It was a terrible wet day when I got married. A wet grey day in 1974 and I couldn't get to the church for the road blocks. I was standing out on my step there with my Mammy screaming at me to come in before I got my good white dress dirty from the rain...only I was wetter from crying than the clouds could make me because Michael Donnelly was the only boy I'd *ever* wanted for myself and me just seventeen he was the only boy I'd wanted at all and it was still a miracle to me he wanted me back...but then since I've always had to

31

work hardest at believing miracles and anyway I knew they only fall in the laps of the pure in heart now...it seemed certain to me that a pile of Brits and a road block would lose me Michael altogether...for why would he wait an hour or more at the church when he'd that smile on him that made you feel wicked and glad about it and that look to him that caught your eye when he was walking down the streets, just with the way he put his feet down, bold and happy together, and those hands that were so warm and gentle you hardly worried where he was putting them and why would a man like that wait two hours in a cold church for a wee girl in a damp wedding dress?

And my Mammy's trying to pull my Daddy in 'cause he's shouting at the Brits saying this was the greatest day of his daughter's life and hadn't they just spoiled it altogether? Then this big Saracen's pulled up and they've all jumped out and my Mammy's just going to scream when do they not offer us an escort through the road block? So that was my bridal car to the wedding, a big Saracen full of Brits all grinning and offering us fags and pleased as punch with themselves for the favour they were doing us. I hardly dared look at them. I was certain the big hulk sitting next to me was one of them that had lifted Michael just the year before but oh they were nice as anything.

There was wanted men at the wedding and everything. Sure I'd grey hairs before I was ever married.

And then I was married and Michael brought me here and the rain stopped, it even looked like the sun had come out and I stared and stared, just standing at the top of the path in my wee white dress that was still half soaked. It felt like we'd won through everything, the weather and the road blocks and the Brits and there were never going to be bad times again...because I was never going to be without him again. Well...I was just seventeen after all.

CHAPTER TWELVE: THE FROG by John Pielmeier

CAROL, a teenager who can't keep her mouth shut, watches her friend, Judy, dissect a frog, a task she finds too repulsive to perform. Carol is changing her blouse under her lab coat.

SCENE: A high school biology lab.

TIME: The present.

CAROL: It's a double date, see? I'm going out with Earl's brother Merle, and Merle won't go out with me unless I find a date for Earl. So if you don't go out with Earl, I don't go out with Merle, and Roger doesn't see Merle and me together and get jealous! [JUDY: Why do you want him to get jealous?] So we can make up and go out together again. God, we had this fight last week, see, Roger and I was watching this movie on TV and it starred Annette Funicello—she's this old-time movie star?—and all he could talk about was her body. So I said, I got a body too you know, which was a big mistake cause then he started talking about *my* body. He *loves* sardines, see, and he said he wanted to pour sardine juice all over my front and lick it off. I practically threw up. And *he* thought it was romantic. I smelled like a fish for days. Oh my God, what's that? [JUDY: The liver. *(Carol takes off her socks and puts on a pair of panty hose.)*] Roger made me eat raw liver at the slaughter house, it was the grossest thing I ever put in my mouth. Well, almost. Anyway, we had this fight after the sardines, so just to make him jealous I decided to go out with this guy from India or Pakistani or some place like that, and he gets over to my house and I always thought them Indians were so quiet and polite and no sooner did we sit down when he pulled his wiener out. Well, I took one look at that little thing and I told him, I said I got a sausage link been setting in my mother's refrigerator for five weeks looks better than that. Ooooh, what's that? [JUDY: The stomach.] *(She can't take her eyes off it.)* Oh, that's so disgusting I think I'm gonna puke. So anyway I kicked him out and now I need to find someone else to make Roger jealous and Merle is perfect 'cause he's so good-looking, even if he is attached to Earl. [JUDY: Attached?] At the hip. What are you doing? [JUDY: Cutting the stomach open. You mean they're physically attached.] That's why I need a double date. Why are you cutting the stomach open? [JUDY: 'Cause we're supposed to see what's inside. Are you telling me they're Siamese twins?] Isn't that fun? Roger'll be *double* jealous. What is it? [JUDY: Flies.] Oh, gross. Roger made me eat a fly once. On Monday Roger ate a spider right before my very eyes. [JUDY: Will you shut up about Roger?!] *(Taken aback.)* God. O-kaaaay. *(For the first time, silence. After a moment, Carol starts searching in her purse.)* You got a baggie? [JUDY: Huh?] To put those legs in. The French eat 'em all the time. [JUDY: You can't eat these legs, they're pickled.] They're not for me, they're for...*(Catching herself, then silently mouthing the forbidden name.)*...Roger. He'll *love* 'em. Hey, want some M&M's? *(She pulls out a bag of M&M's.)*

COFFEE AFTER THE STORM by Lavonne Mueller

OLIVE WIGGINS, just home from Desert Storm, considers herself a hero.

SCENE: A coffee shop.

TIME: Shortly after Operation Desert Storm.

OLIVE: *(Speaking to an unseen waiter:)* Coffee. With cream.
(She slaps money on the counter.)
Yah.....yah. I was in Saudi.
(She drinks)
What?
Sure I'm a real Corporal. You're not the only one to ask me that. A lot of pople want to know what it's like being a woman soldier. Are you a token, they ask? A puppet? A crumb thrown in the mouth of war? Well, I'm as much a warrior as Ike....... Westmoreland....... Schwarzkopf..... or any of the others.
(She salutes the waiter. She holds the salute.)
The name's Corporal Olive....... Olive for peace, Wiggins.
(She drops the salute.)
I used to date some Arab from Paw Paw, Illinois, before the war. Bahiaddin Ali Faris Ketsaraa Abdul Chucheep. I called him Dul for short. He worked in a Taco Bell at the I-94 Truck Plaza, and he always gave me free coffee even before we started going out. Dul was really nice for an Arab. He didn't wear a dish-rag with tassels on his head or do chants from one of them parachute towers. You know, pretty ordinary. He did have a "prayer bump" just below his hairline from pressing his forehead to the ground in pious meditation. I got him to wear his bushy eyebrows combed up over it so nobody could really

34

tell. And occasionally I'd get aggravated with the "Mecca indicator" on the ceiling of his Honda. We'd go for a simple drive in the country............ and this fancy compass gadget kept reminding us which way to bow our heads in prayer when Dul didn't even have automatic shift.

Dul was sweet, though. He gave me a tape of Bluegrass II for my birthday. With the war and all, he's not at Taco Bell anymore and I wouldn't wanna get it on with him now, anyway. But sometimes when I was walking in the Kurdistan mountains dodging our own A-V8 jump jets or in the desert with a full moon out feeling lonely with only camels and cute little oil-slicked cormorants, I'd think of him.

I was proud to be in Saudi on the historic day the war started. I was PX Supply Clerk at the time. It was my job to help our Saudi allies understand instructions on various boxes and jars of stuff given out freely by Special Services. I didn't spead Arabic, of course. And none of them Gulfies spoke English. But it was my lucky break to act-out how to use a hemorrhoid suppository for a member of the Afghan Mujahedeen. I want to tell you that Afghan was so grateful he gave me the helmet of a dead Colonel from the Republican Guard. I got it hanging up under my Elk's head in my kitchen in Shabonna.

This high-impact magic marker I wear around my neck was used for bomb-signing. The men wrote their thing on a bomb or missile, whatever, and then their personalized weapon was forklifted across a pontoon bridge to me in a quonset at the Port of Jubail. "Cram-it Saddam it." Stuff like that. I went over each word carefully in permanent black. Then I signed my own name like the famous painter Norman Rockwell. It was very spiritual to think of my "name" maybe slamming into Tikrit, Hussein's home town, and his fory wives diving under a prayer mat for cover. You know, like *them* blasting Kennebunkport.

Don't think I was in the rear. I want you to understand there were a lot of missiles and 50-caliber tracers around me all the time. Of course no real people got wasted. Just....... Sheiks, bedouins, Ottoman......................... stuff like that. It got kind of bloody sometimes. I've seen a lot of death. And I want to tell you, the Iraqi give off the yip of a dying dog. Death for a pagan is not quiet.

Well, I gotta get up early. I'm being air-lifted to the Strait of

Hormuz tomorrow. To a huge desalting plant. The Army feels all that discarded salt can be stockpiled in case we go to war with another one of them Mesopotamian countries. Putting salt back in the enemy's drinking water is okay by the Geneva Convention.

I'll probably be back in Illinois in a year or so. No doubt you'll see me driving around DeKalb County in one of my Humvees. Thank god around here you can always pull any time into a station for gas as nobody in this country closes in the middle of the day for prayer.

(*A beat as she responds to the waiter*) Oh, I'll be glad to give you an autograph. It'll be fun to sign a napkin for a change. I'll even use my bomb-marker. (*Saying as she signs:*) Corporal..... Olive..... Olive for Peace Wiggins. (*Hands napkin to the waiter and exits.*)

CREDO by Craig Lucas

A lone PERSON speaks.

SCENE: Uncertain.

TIME: Unknown.

(*Lights up. Person alone on stage.*)

PERSON:

So it's Christmas eve,
I go out with the dog.
Jim and I have just broken up.
I've just been to an AA meeting
Where a woman got up
And said she had no friends,
Her best friend is her VCR
And it's broken.
I came home to the hole where the sofa was.
There's no Christmas tree either.
I can't stand the thought of sweeping up all the dead needles
And dragging the carcass out to the street
To join all the other dead trees

36

With what's happening to the rain forest.
I know the two aren't connected,
But anyway, I pull up a folding chair
And heat up a piece of cold pizza.
This, I think, is the low point.
The walls show little ghosts where the pictures once were.
I go out.

Did I tell you I didn't get my Christmas bonus?
Well, I wasn't expecting it,
But I haven't been able to take Apple to the vet about her problem,
So she dribbles a little across the lobby,
Past the doorman who isn't smiling at me;
I'm sure it's because I haven't given him *his* Christmas bonus,
But maybe it's the trail of urine, too,
I don't stop to ask.
I smile bravely
And step outside where it has of course started to rain.
And people are running and looking very upset.
Surely the rain isn't that bad.
I turn:
There's been an accident on my corner.
I snap my head away,
I know if I look there'll be a baby carriage there
In the middle of the street.
I refuse to look.
They certainly don't need another person standing around, not doing
    anything.
I put my mind…Where can I put my mind?
Vienna.
Where Jim has gone with the woman he left me for.
You can't escape these thoughts.
All I know is her name.
Her name…is Carmella.
Apparently.
And I believe that she has had a sex change.
As far as I know, this has no basis in fact,

But I believe it as firmly as I believe
We are all headed straight to hell
If the Republicans spend one more minute
In the White House.

Where,
Where can I put my thoughts?
Ecuador.
My parents are in Ecuador.
They asked me to join them,
And I said
No, Jim and I would be spending the holiday together.
I hope that he and Carmella are caught
In the crossfire of some [terrorist]...
No, I don't.
Not really. But you know:
The sort of thing you see
On the evening news.
If you have a TV.
Or a phone.
Jim stopped paying the bills months ago,
As a kind of secret warning of what was to come.
But I refuse,
In my bones I refuse
To see myself as a victim.
I have gotten myself into this.
I allowed him to talk me into maintaining a joint bank account.
Every time a little voice in my head would say
Watch out.
He's cute,
But he's not that nice.
Beneath it all,
Behind the charm,
His chin,
That first night,
And then again in Barbados,
Beneath it all

Is *him.*
I alone took each and every step
Which brought me here
To this street corner
In the rain
On Christmas eve
With my dog whose urinary infection
I cannot afford to fix.
And at that moment, my friends,
My dog squats,
And the worst thing that has ever happened to me
Unfolds before my very eyes.
A wire, a loose plug from somebody's Christmas decorations
Carelessly strung in front of their little tea shop...
Electrocutes my dog.
And she falls immediately dead
On the sidewalk
In a sputter of sparks...
And the lights go out all down the front of the tea shop.
And a man comes out:
"What did you do?"
And I drop to my knees, unafraid,
Let me die, too,
Electrocute me.
And I embrace my dog, Apple,
Whom I have had for sixteen years.
She is my oldest friend.
She has seen me in my darkest, most drunken days.
She has been to every corner of my life, watched me make love.
She growled at the dogs on the dogfood commercials.
She has been across the country and back.
Apple, I'm not afraid to say, is the purest,
Most uncomplicated expression of love I have ever known.
And she has been killed by an electric current
In the last sick days of her valiant existence.

The man stares at me from above.

"Oh my god" he says.
He can't believe it
Any more than I can believe it.
Come in, he says.
We carry Apple into the shop.
To me she smells good,
But to some people she does not.
It's been too cold to bathe her.
It's hard for one person to hold her in the shower.
She doesn't like the water.

The man offers me the only thing he has.
Tea.
We talk,
And he assures me that the accident on the corner
Did *not* involve a child.
And no one was killed.

What to do now with Apple?
I can't cry anymore.
I have cried so much the last two weeks
I can't cry for her now.
And I know...
In some way I see all at once that
Jim was not really good enough for me,
That I will meet someone else.
And even if I don't I will have
An extraordinary and rich and complicated life.
It is entirely up to me.
I will most likely survive all the roadblocks and the detours.
As my dad always says:
"Life can be rough, but think about the alternative."

But then again
He's never been sick a day in his life.
He hasn't ever had to struggle just to stand
Or been unable to stop himself from peeing

Where he knows he shouldn't
And doesn't want to,
But there it is in a stream,
Surprising him and me.
He's never had to look up
With big sorrowful eyes which say:
"I had no idea.
I know this is wrong.
Don't yell."

No.
I only hope that I will go as quickly as Apple
When the time comes.
And if I don't,
I will absolutely,
I *know* I will face that bravely
And with dignity.
I know.
And if,
For some unforeseen but totally justified reason,
I can't,
And I am making a complete ass of myself,
Saying things I wouldn't ever say
And acting childishly
And turning into a prude
And a conservative
And am being a complete drag on everyone
For months and years,
I know my friends will forgive me.
And if for some equally valid and twisted,
But ultimately logical reason,
They don't,
Or they can't,
Or they're all dead by then,
Or it's August and they're away,
Then I will forgive them,
Right?

The same way I forgave myself
For yelling at Apple the first time she peed
Before I realized what was going on.

And if...
Again, if I can't,
And everything is entirely for shit
And I can't even find my way to the end of a sentence...
And...you can fill in all the blanks...

That will be fine, too.

DANCING AT LUGHNASA by Brian Friel

The story of two days in the life of the five Mundy sisters who live in County Donegal, Ireland in 1936.

Lughnasa (loo-na-sa) is the feast day of the Irish god Lugh.

MAGGIE, thirty-eight, the housekeeper for her working sisters, recalls a time long ago when she participated in a dance contest. The memory surfaces when she hears that her childhood girlfriend, Bernie O'Donnel has come back for a visit, married and the mother of twins. And they won't be seeing each other.

SCENE: The kitchen of their house.

TIME: 1936. Harvest time.

MAGGIE: When I was sixteen I remember slipping out one Sunday night—it was this time of year, the beginning of August—and Bernie and I met at the gate of the workhouse and the pair of us off to a dance in Ardstraw. I was being pestered by a fellow called Tim Carlin at the time but it was really Brian McGuinness that I was—that I was keen on. Remember Brian with the white hands and the longest eyelashes you ever saw? But of course he was crazy about Bernie. Anyhow the two boys took us on the bar of their bikes and off the four of us headed to Ardstraw, fifteen miles each way. If Daddy had known, may he rest in peace...

And at the end of the night there was a competition for the Best Military Two-step. And it was down to three couples: the local pair from Ardstraw; wee Timmy and myself—he was up to there on me; and Brian and Bernie...

And they were just so beautiful together, so stylish; you couldn't take your eyes off them. People just stopped dancing and gazed at them...

And when the judges announced the winners—they were probably blind drunk—naturally the local couple came first; and Timmy and myself came second; and Brian and Bernie came third.

Poor Bernie was stunned. She couldn't believe it. Couldn't talk. Wouldn't speak to any of us for the rest of the night. Wouldn't even cycle home with us. She was right, too: they should have won; they were just so beautiful together...

And that's the last time I saw Brian McGuinness—remember Brian with the...? And the next thing I heard he had left for Australia...

She was right to be angry, Bernie. I know it wasn't fair—it wasn't fair at all. I mean they must have been blind drunk, those judges, whoever they were...

DEARLY DEPARTED by David Botrell and Jessie Jones

When Bud Turpin dies, his entire clan comes to the funeral. In a car, Bud's son, Junior and his wife, SUZANNE, in her twenties, are having an argument. Their kids are in the back seat.

SCENE: In and around the towns of Lula and Timson, somewhere below the Mason-Dixon line. The Turpins' car.

TIME: The present.

SUZANNE: How's she gonna go on? That's what I'd like to know. How's she gonna face life without Daddy-Bud. I just don't know how she's gonna go on without losing her mind.

(She waits for a response but doesn't get one)

43

Well, I can't decide what to sing. Of course, I don't know how I'll get through it. I swear to God, I don't. I'll probably just fall down on the floor in a big pool of tears. God knows nobody would blame me if I did. All our humiliation and now Daddy Bud has to up and die without seeing you make something of yourself.

[JUNIOR: Maybe you could sing "Jesus on the Cross."]

I don't know. That doesn't seem sad enough for a funeral. And God knows it's gonna be sad to be sitting there thinking how your Daddy died knowing we had to sell everything we owned and move into that God-awful trailer just to pay off that big dream of yours.

[JUNIOR: Maybe you could set that to music, Suzanne.]

I believe I was just stating the facts, wasn't I? You know I loved him too, Junior. He was just like my own Daddy. I was the one that had to go crawling to him like a snake and beg for the money to buy shoes for our children, you know. But I did it. I humbled myself. And do you know why I did it, Junior? It can all be summed up in two little words: "for love."

(Suddenly slapping "the children" over the backseat)

I TOLD YOU TO STOP KICKING THE BACK OF MY SEAT! I Know You're Hungry! You Think I'm Not? It'd Be Nice To Stop And Get Something To Eat, Wouldn't It? Maybe We Could If Your Daddy Hadn't Lost All Our Money!

Love, Junior. That's been the curse of my life. And now we have to face your family with all of them knowing. All of them looking down on us, laughing at us. Who ever heard of a machine that cleans parking lots.

[JUNIOR: That'll do, Suzanne.]

All our money down the toilet, Junior. How do you feel about that? You think I like working at Newberry's? Slaving to keep that wax fruit section looking nice. You think I wouldn't love to stay home and watch soap operas all day like my good for nothing sisters do. That would suit me just fine, mister. Let me tell you that right now. I don't want to work, I have to. I'd love to stay home and keep a decent house, cook for you, maybe learn to sew and make some clothes for the children. That's all I ever wanted to be was just a good wife and mother.

(Suddenly slapping "the children" again)

44

YOU DO THAT AGAIN AND I'm gonna tell your Daddy to pull this car over and throw you all out in the road! How would you like us to put you out in the road and just drive off and never look back? Then what would you do with no mother and daddy to look after you? Starve! Starve to death in the road.

(She settles back into her seat, returns to her music)

Go on and cry, you big babies.

(Pause)

[JUNIOR: *(over his shoulder, quietly)* Y'all know your mama loves you. She was just kidding.]

We'll see who's kidding. Don't miss this turn off. I just don't know how they expect me to stand up there and sing. I don't know how I'll do it.

[JUNIOR: I'm sure you'll do your best.]

My best? That's a good one. You don't know a thing about it Junior. In order to do my best, I'd have to have confidence. I used to have confidence. I used to think the world was my oyster. I could have married Sylvester Banks and had a big house on a hill. But, no. I could have gone to college. Could have had a career. But no, I couldn't think of myself. That's been my curse my whole life. I never once thought of myself. I had to listen to my foolish heart and get married to a dreamer. A beautiful dreamer who goes out an blows all our money on a big piece of machinery to clean parking lots.

[JUNIOR: You're pushing it.]

Did you ever once stop to think that maybe nobody gave a damn about a clean parking lot.

[JUNIOR: You're really pushing it.]

And of course, it came as a big surprise to you when everbody just laughed in your face when you asked them if they wanted their parking lot cleaned.

DEATH AND THE MAIDEN by Ariel Dorfman

PAULINA ESCOBAR, around forty, was a victim of torture during the previous regime. Paulina thinks she recognizes the voice of her torturer when her husband brings home a stranger, DR. JORGE MIRANDA.

45

Miranda stays for the night, during which Paulina ties him up. When he awakes, he's staring into the face of Paulina and a gun. To save his life, he must confess to being her torturer, so he does. The question remains: is he telling the truth? Paulina's torturer would incessantly play Shubert's "Death and the Maiden" while he worked.

SCENE: A country that is probably Chile but could be any country that has given itself a democratic government just after a long period of dictatorship. The Escobar beach house by the sea.

TIME: The present.

PAULINA: Good morning, Doctor...Miranda, isn't it? Doctor Miranda.

(She shows him the gun and points it playfully in his direction.)

You wouldn't be related to the Mirandas of San Fernando, would you? I had a chum from the University, name of Miranda, Ana Maria Miranda, Anita had quite a mind, prodigious memory, we used to call her our little encyclopaedia, I have no idea what's become of her, she must have ended up as a doctor just like you did, right? I never finished my career in medicine, Doctor Miranda. Let's see if you can guess why I never finished my career in medicine, why I didn't get my diploma, I'm pretty sure that it won't take a colossal effort of the imagination on your part to guess why. But luckily there was Gerardo. He was—well, I wouldn't exactly say he was waiting for me—but let's say that he still loved me, so I never had to go back to the University to finish up. Lucky for me, because I sort of felt—well, phobia is not the right word, a certain apprehension—about my chosen profession. But life is never over till it's over, they say, and that's why I'm wondering whether it might not be a good idea to sign up again—you know, ask that I be readmitted. I read the other day that the University, now that the military aren't in charge anymore, has begun to allow the professors and students who were kicked out to ask for readmittance. But here I am chatting away when I'm supposed to make breakfast, right, a nice breakfast? Now you like—let's see, ham with mayonnaise, wasn't it that, ham with mayonnaise and tomato sandwiches, that was it—we haven't got mayonnaise, but we do have ham, Gerardo also likes ham. Soon I'll get to know your other tastes. I

46

hope you don't mind that this must remain, for the moment, a monologue. You'll have your say, Doctor, you can be sure I'll let you have your say. It's just that for the moment I'd rather not take off this—gag, you call it, don't you?—at least not till Gerardo wakes up. And as the AAA truck is coming by soon.

(She goes to the bedroom door, unlocks it, opens it.)

In fact, it's about time he got up.

The real real truth is that you look slightly bored. While I make you a nice breakfast—because I do happen to have milk—what if we listen to some Schubert. *Death and the Maiden?*

(She goes to the cassette-player and puts in a cassette. We begin to hear Schubert's quartet Death and the Maiden.*)*

D'you know how long it's been since I haven't listened to this quartet? If it's on the radio, I switch it off, I even try not to go out much, though Gerardo has all these social events he's got to attend and if they ever name him Minister we're going to live running around shaking hands and smiling at perfect strangers, but I always pray they won't put on Schubert, one night we were dining with—they were extremely important people, and our hostess happened to put Schubert on, a piano sonata, and I thought, do I switch it off or do I leave, but my body decided for me, I felt extremely ill right then and there and Gerardo had to take me home, so we left them there listening to Schubert and nobody knew what had made me ill, so I pray they won't play that anywhere I go, any Schubert at all, strange isn't it, when he used to be, and I would say, yes I really would say, he's still my favorite composer, such a sad, noble sense of life. But I always promised myself a time would come to recover him, bring him back from the grave so to speak, and just sitting here listening to him with you I know that I was right, that I'm—so many things that are going to change from now on, right? To think I was on the verge of throwing my whole Schubert collection out, crazy, huh? And now I'll be able to listen to my Schubert again, even go to a concert like we used to before I—Did you know that Schubert was homosexual? But of course you do, you're the one who kept repeating that information in my ear so many times, precisely while you played *Death and the Maiden.* Is this the very cassette, Doctor, or do you buy a new one every year so the sound can remain—pristine? On target?

47

(She goes to the bedroom door and speaks to GERARDO.)
You've got to get up, Gerardo. The AAA will be here at any minute. Isn't this quartet marvelous, my love?

DEFYING GRAVITY by Jane Anderson

ELIZABETH, thirty, recalls the events leading up to her mother's death twenty-five years before as an astronaut in an ill-fated space shot. She speaks to the audience from an unspecified location.

TIME: The near future.

ELIZABETH: I remember a *reporter* asked me what I thought of my mother going into space. I didn't want to answer so I hid my face behind my grandmother's purse. My brother laughed at me so I hit him on the arm. My grandmother gave us Lifesavers to quiet us down. I told her I wanted a cherry so she peeled the paper down until she found one for me. I put it in my pocket for later. Then my mother joined us and she let me hold her hand while she talked to the reporters. I played with her wedding ring and I was very proud that I was one of the few people who was allowed to touch her hand. She showed the reporters some of the things she was taking up to space. She had a journal and in the journal was a bookmark that I made for her. I had drawn a rocket and stars and Saturn with the rings and I ironed it between two pieces of wax paper so it would be protected from the gamma rays. Then she showed the reporters something her class had given her. I was jealous and I wanted to give her something else. So I took out the Lifesaver. It was fuzzy from the lining of my pocket. While my mother and the reporters talked, I tried to make the Lifesaver presentable. I told myself that I had to pick all the lint off the Lifesaver or my mother wouldn't come back. Finally my mother crouched down next to me. She was wearing her blue space suit. I touched the patches on her shoulders. She looked so beautiful. Suddenly I couldn't grasp that this woman was the same person who every morning sliced banana on my granola. My grandmother kept saying, "say goodbye, honey, say goodbye to your mother." But all I

48

could manage to do was to hold out the Lifesaver which was sticky from the sweat of my hand. My mother took it and put it in her pocket and I knew that everything would be all right.

When I watched my mother's ship take off, I saw it go straight into the sky and disappear. When my grandmother told me that my mother went to heaven, I thought that heaven was a part of outer space. I was excited because I thought she'd come back with all kinds of neat presents like a plastic harp or a pair of angel wings. I went to the mail box every day looking for a post card from her that would have clouds on it or a three-D picture of God. I waited for her to call long distance. When I didn't hear from her, I got very angry. I told my father that I hated her for being away so long. He told me that she had "perished" in the rocket. I told him that wasn't true, that she was alive. That she had left us and found a family that she liked better. He asked me why did I think she was still alive. And I said, "because I never saw her dead." These are the reasons I gave myself for why my mother didn't come back. One: I hit my brother on the arm. Two: I wouldn't talk to the reporters. Three: I didn't say thank you to my Grandma for giving me the coloring book. Four: I wouldn't let my father hold me. Five: I didn't get all the lint off the Lifesaver.

EARTH AND SKY by Doug Post

SARA McKEON is a poet in her twenties who works in a library. David, the man she loves, has been found brutally murdered. The police attribute his death to the secret life they claim David led—a life which involved him in rape, murder, kidnapping, and heroin. But Sara cannot accept that the man she knew was the monster the police describe. She has begun her own investigation. Her friend and the police tell her she is in danger and order her to stop. Here—in a combination of two speeches—she explains to her friend, Joyce, and a friendly bartender why she must go on.

SCENE: A bar.

TIME: The present.

SARA: I am sick of being hidden! I am fed up with behaving

49

well! I am so tired of fear and ignorance and the feeling in my gut of utter uselessness! I hate this state! This dream state I've created! I close up! I hear nothing! I see some kind of a perfect world which exists nowhere I can find! AND I'M DONE WITH IT! *(Pause.)* A man died. I thought I knew him. I continue to love him. And I will see this through. To my own end. To the end of my belief. *(Pause.)* He was kind to me. He listened when I spoke. He saw me and not the illusion I create. He understood my scribblings and read them again and again. He held me in the dark when I needed reassurance. He was the childhood I never had. The good death I dream of. He was my own life. My heart. My breath. My skin and bones. All of my sins and aspirations. Heaven and earth. Earth and sky.

EMOTIONAL RECALL by John Pielmeier

An ACTRESS speaks to the audience.

ACTRESS: Let me tell you about my father's death.
I was only five.
It was in a field, on our farm, and I'd been playing in a tree when it started to rain. My father came to bring me home, first calling me from across the field, and I didn't come, and the rain fell heavier and harder, and he walked to the middle of the field, calling and I didn't come, even though I heard him I didn't come, and he came closer, three-quarters of the way through the wheat, calling me, "Please, *(Actress' name)*, come home," and I didn't come, and I didn't come, and then
there was brightness
incredible light
and my father was a torch
screaming
and I called to him
"Daddy! Daddy!"
and he didn't come
and he didn't come.
(She is crying She stops, recovers.)
Let me tell you about my father's death.

I was three-and-a-half.

It was in a field, on our farm, and I'd been playing in a tree when it started to snow. My father came to bring me home, and I didn't come, and the snow fell, and he walked to the middle of the field, and I didn't come, and he walked slower and slower, and I wouldn't come, and he froze, all blue, solid ice, and...

(She is crying. She stops, recovers.)

Let me tell you about my father's death.

My mother was eight months pregnant, and they were in a field, a big wide field, and it was night, and suddenly there was this huge light, falling from the heavens, it was a space ship, and it fell on my father, and it squashed him...flat...like a pancake...and my mother...who always liked pancakes...

(She can't go on. She is crying. She stops.)

A wild elephant came racing across the ice. My father, fishing, didn't see him, and...

(She is crying.)

An invisible force drew him to the house, where the ghost of his fiancee, hungry for blood, was...

(She is sobbing.)

A wild Chinaman, an escapee from Devil's Island...

(She has lost control.)

I'm sorry. I'm sorry.

(She regains control, composes herself.)

Let me tell you about my father's death.

He was an acting teacher.

Mad for emotional honesty.

He drove his students to the edge.

Over, if necessary.

They loved him for that.

It has to be real, he said. Even the silliest, most impossible situation, you have to believe it. Dig into your heart. If you don't have a dead parent, use a dead pet.

He was a pusher for honesty. Honesty was his drug.

I suppose he pushed Ellen too far.

Tell us about your father's death, he said one day in class.

No, she said.

Do you remember?
No.
Were you there?
No.
You're lying. Tell us. Tell us, Ellen! You wanted him dead, didn't you?! You wished him dead, didn't you?!
I don't know what you're talking about, she said.
Next day, he took a new approach.
Did he do something bad to you?
No, she said.
Don't be ashamed, Ellen. Don't be afraid.
I'm not.
You are! Face the facts about him! Face the ugly, dirty, smelly, disgusting truth! You'll never be an actress if you can't face the truth! Did he hate you?! Hit you?! Worse?!!
I don't know what you're talking about, she said. I wish you'd leave me alone.
Next day he took a new approach.
So did she.
I'm your father, he said. Did you love me?
No answer.
Did you hate me?
No answer.
Did you feel anything?! Only dead things don't feel! Are you dead, Ellen?! ARE YOU DEAD?!!!
No, you are, she said, and shot him.
Turns out she never even knew her father. She just didn't like people shouting.
And the amazing thing is that I saw it all.
The gun, the pop, the blood.
Dad screaming.
It was pretty awful.
I don't like to think about it.
Let me tell you about my puppy's death.
He was just a little thing, and this...this witch, from the gingerbread cottage down the road...
(She is sobbing. She stops, recovers.)
Let me try that again.

(Blackout.)

52

THE EXTRA MAN by Richard Greenberg

LAURA, married and in her twenties, has just ended her affair with a male friend. She is packing her things in his apartment. A couple who know about the affair have just snubbed her in Central Park.

SCENE: A New York City apartment.

TIME: The present.

LAURA: *(starts to fold and pack the clothing arrayed on the bed)*: I... *(A moment, tries again, effortfully casual)* I ran into Paula yesterday. At the place in the park we used to go because nobody else ever did. She was there with Randy. I'd always thought she disliked Randy, didn't you? But from the looks of things, they must have become friends. I hadn't seen them in ages...I hadn't really wanted to...but when they were walking towards me, I had...I felt the strangest...this completely unexpected *joy*... this wild, I don't know, *relief*...like when someone dies in your dream and you finally wake up. They were laughing very hard at something and they didn't see me at first and I guess I sort of rushed at them...and then they did see me. And they stopped laughing...together...as though they'd planned it. They didn't say anything. *(Beat. She stops folding clothes; resumes)* Which seemed...peculiar. So I said, "Hello, isn't it a nice day?" "Funny," Paula said, "We were just remarking that it *wasn't*." She seemed really adamant about that; I'd never seen anyone in quite such a huff about the weather before. So I didn't know what to say next because if you can't talk about the weather, well then, I mean, what's left? No one spoke for about a year until Randy saved us by piping up: "If we don't hurry, we'll be inexcusably late. "Oh, go," I said, "Christ, don't be inexcusably late—where are you going, anyway?" "To friends," Paula said. "We're going to see friends." And they nodded and moved on—neither of them uttering a word until I was well out of earshot, at which point they became quite animated. *(Beat.)* Talking.

A GATHERING OF NETTLES by Nathan Eldon Sanders

FAYE, thirties, believes the Martians are coming for her tomorrow, but first plans to kill her sister, Willie, by putting a snake in her hat box. Meantime, however, Willie unexpectedly dies of natural causes. Now Faye mourns her sister and reviews their life together. The Mormon bishop and townspeople are outside waiting to claim Willie's body.

SCENE: The small southern town of Sugar Bean, the sisters' house.

TIME: The present.

FAYE: (*To ROBINELLE*) Hand me Willie's pocket book over yonderways...Willie'd never forgive me if I let the Bishop Crumley see her without making her up as pretty as possible...

(*FAYE applies lipstick to WILLIE's cold lips*)

There...see, just a little dab...I've always thought Willie was so pretty...Here...and we'll straighten her wig a little...there. Perfect. Perfect as can be...(*Touching WILLIE's face*) I know why you always walked three steps ahead of me on the way to school, Willie. You didn't want nobody in Sugar Bean to think we was related. (*Starts to laugh*) Remember that day on the playground when we was eating lunch...and Fanny Alridge come running over to us talking a mile a minute...and the whole while she had this great, big green snot booger just a' hanging out her nose...and when she breathed it come poking out even further...and I got to laughing so hard I was farting and pissing in my drawers and my nut-butter and jelly-jam samich come shooting out my nose! And all the youngins come over...and they started laughing at me! And remember what you done, Willie? Remember what you done?! You come over and started laughing right along with them. Laughing at me. So they wouldn't laugh at you. You didn't have to be ashamed of me, Willie. I just wanted you to be my sister. I just wanted you to love me the way I always loved you.

(*FAYE leaves WILLIE's body*)

(*To ROBINELLLE*) Alright. Open it. But tell them first...tell them first that they got to be real careful with Willie when they carry her out. They can't bang her into the walls and bruise her or drop her or anything. They got to be real gentle with her. They are gonna treat her right. And with respect! And they ain't to laugh at her. Even if her wig comes off her head when they carry her out. They ain't gonna laugh at Willie. I just ain't gonna have it. I don't never want nobody to laugh at Willie.

(*FAYE crossed and sits in Mama's rocker*)
Let them in...

GENERATIONS OF THE DEAD IN THE ABYSS OF CONEY ISLAND MADNESS by Michael Henry Brown

The play centers around LENORE and her twin children—Reed and Lena. Lenore, a black woman, around thirty-four, makes Ma Barker look benign. She encourages Lena to marry an ineffectual man named Cody because he has a wealthy mother. She has a husband she cheats on with a drug pusher and she causes her son, filled with hatred for her, to blind himself. She also watches a couple of murders with equanimity.

Here, she answers Reed, who bitterly wonders why she gave him and Lena away at their birth.

SCENE: An apartment in the Poseidon housing projects in the Coney Island section of Brooklyn.

TIME: The present.

LENORE: What?...I was fifteen years old, what was I supposed to do?
[REED: Chill?]
While your father ran around the country?...What the fuck did I need him for? He wasn't there for me. So I went out there and made my own money. Nigger wasn't making shit. What did I need with a broke sax player? That's what I thought as I laid there in labor...laid there thinking it was all over....They hung that little bitch upside down and smacked her on the ass, and shit, I'm relieved...ready for them to wheel me out...shit yeah!...Then the doctor says, "Brace yourself,

55

here comes another." Motherfucker, you almost killed me. I was just a little thing. All by myself. Where the fuck was that dope-shootin' sax-playin' father of yours? I couldn't call my mother, God rest her soul, she had tried her best to stomp you and your sister out of me... (*Silence*) Never saw you come out. Woke up and it was three days later. I had hemorrhaged. Where the fuck was he? Blowin' that sax in a shootin' gallery in west hell? See, a nigger can't be there when I need him, then I don't need the son of a bitch. (*REED tries to turn on the T.V. She slaps his hand*) I laid there thinkin' of how I almost died alone 'cause I believed in some fairy-tale/prince-charming/mother-goose-you-in-the-ass bullshit. And I swore to myself I wouldn't be this fool again, not in this life....So I was ripe when your father's mother and sister came to my hospital bed and said they'd take the both of you.

[REED: The faithful wait.

LENORE: The suckers wait.

REED: How would you know? You never waited.

LENORE: What was I supposed to wait for?

REED: Something real.]

It don't get no more real than this. (*REED tries to turn on the T.V. She slaps his hand again*) If you listen to me, I'd set you straight about survival....This ain't Long Island...this is Coney Island.

[REED: I'm going to find my own island...]

Where are you going to go? Before you and Lena decided to live with me, you didn't know a thing. You were both just like that Cody...spoilt brats....But who hipped you? Who taught you the real deal? (*REED points to her*) So you admit it. (*REED covers his ears*) Then why do you and your sister act like you're better than me?

[REED: It's your imagination.]

I ain't never had any use for imagination. You and your sister ain't no better than me and the rest of my kids. Just remember, you sprang from me, bitch....So if you think I'm shit...

[REED: I'm shit?]

(*Pause*) You got that right. (*She goes to the dinette table and picks up the vial of coke*) You're right here in the shit with me...I'm your blood. (*REED watches her as she goes to the window and looks out*) Hot as a son of a bitch...

GENTILE OF THE TOP PERCENTILE by Bruce E. Whitacre

Teenage REVA is trying to find a way of living with her eccentric father, a former business executive who has turned his back on the world and lives as an eighteenth-century gentleman in contemporary New York, complete with candlelight, quill pens, servants, and carriages.

SCENE: A New York City apartment.

TIME: The present.

REVA: You really want to know what I want, Dad? Put on a pair of pants and take me to Four Seasons for lunch. Just like the good old days, just like real life. I mean, what's the big deal? What has happened to my parents? Stella and Lloyd think Radio Shack is the doorway to heaven. And look at you—knee pants, that powdered wig, ink stains on your fingers—is normalcy too much to ask? Don't get me wrong. I'm glad you tried—you know—to take me in and everything. But I want to get a job, pay some bills, make some friends, live. You see what I mean? Have a real life. I'm ready but I don't know how. I need someone to talk to, help me get started. I need a Dad, not a Pappa.

GETTING TO KNOW JEWS by Douglas Bernstein and Denis Markell

ELLEN FOLEY has married into a Jewish family whose traditions she is beginning to learn.

ELLEN: *(spoken intro:)* As you just heard, my name is Ellen Foley. Actually, since I've been married, I have a new name: Ellen Foley Bernstein. My name isn't the only change I've made since then. I've learned so very much...*(She sings:)*

IT'S A VERY ANCIENT SAYING, BUT A TRUE AND HONEST

THOUGHT
FROM THE MOMENT THAT YOU'RE MARRIED—
BY YOUR NEW IN-LAWS YOU'LL BE TAUGHT
AS A NEW BRIDE I'VE BEEN LEARNING (YOU'LL FORGIVE
    ME IF I BOAST)
AND I'VE NOW BECOME AN EXPERT ON A SUBJECT I LIKE
    MOST...

GETTING TO KNOW JEWS—GETTING TO KNOW ALL ABOUT
    JEWS
GETTING TO LIKE JEWS—GETTING TO HOPE JEWS LIKE ME
GETTING TO KNOW JEWS—PUTTING IT THEIR WAY, SO
    NICELY
THEY ARE PRECISELY MY CUP OF TEA (yes, the cake was
    delicious, I just can't eat another bite!...)

GETTING TO KNOW JEWS—GETTING TO HEAR THINGS LIKE
    KIDDUSH
WHEN I AM WITH JEWS—GETTING TO KNOW WHAT TO SAY
HAVEN'T YOU NOTICED SUDDENLY I'M SPEAKING
    YIDDISH?
LIKE KREPLACH AND FOODS BEAUTIFUL AND NEW
THAT I'M PRACTICING TO CHEW, DAY BY DAY

GETTING TO KNOW JEWS—GETTING TO PEEK AT THE
    TORAH
GETTING TO MEET JEWS—GETTING TO JOIN THE U.J.A.
NEXT TO THE TREE NOW, I HAVE A GREAT BIG MENORAH
AND COUSINS NAMED RUTH, ABRAHAM, AND MILT
I LEARN SO MUCH ABOUT GUILT—DAY BY DAY

GIRL NEXT DOOR by Laurence Klavan

PAGE BAILEY, a cheerful lady in her thirties, has always dreamt of moving to the suburbs, with her husband, Bill. She has finally made it to Leveltown, Long Island and explains to her two neighbors why she's so happy.

58

SCENE: Page's house.

TIME: The present.

PAGE: It was my dream, this house—my dream house. The city was like a pair of crossed legs, all clammy and closed. But out here in the suburbs, those legs parted; there was so much room, so much freedom, your next door neighbor could be a million miles away. Open Legs, Long Island, should be our name. *(They both stifle laughter. PAGE looks at them, a bit confused, hesitant now.)* Well, maybe I went a bit overboard. But I mean it. If you grew up the way I did—five to a room, life shut at the thigh, my father illiterate, good only with his fists, finding a trade at last as a meat tenderizer, proudly pounding his meat until they invented that darned serrated hammer and his career was ruined and he took to drinking and "tenderizing" my mother's face— *(controls herself; then—)* But all that's behind me now. I'm here, only a few minutes from a mall, my man *(checks her watch)* only a few minutes late. The owner of the original Leveltown home.

GIRL NEXT DOOR by Laurence Klavan

JILL DAILEY, in her late twenties, is the slut of the suburbs—Leveltown, Long Island. Men succumb to her obvious availability. Bill Bailey, her next door neighbor, comes over—ostensibly to complain about the loud music she plays. But Jill, smoking as talks, knows better.

SCENE: Jill's house, filled with junk.

TIME: The present.

JILL: No, you didn't. The music wasn't too loud, it was a siren song to you. You came because I reek between the legs, I could bathe all day. Because I can't cook for shit, sometimes I think of little boys naked, and I haven't read anything better than the Cable Guide in years. Because I'm not careful with cash—there are dollar bills like dustballs on my floor and dustballs the size of tumbleweeds. Because I use Kleenex for tampons and Kleenex for napkins. Because I don't use Kleenex; I pick my nose so much I get nosebleeds. Because I shoplift shoelaces from stores. Because sometimes I like to be butt-fucked. *(beat)* Because you're crazy about me. I knew it the first moment you looked at me. It's like on TV: Channel 25 is the preacher, Channel 23 is the porn. We're so much alike: Bill and Jill, Bailey and Dailey, numbers 23 and 25, two letters, two numbers, apart. I was only having Marvin what'shisname because I wasn't having you.

GIRL NEXT DOOR by Laurence Klavan

The neighbors in a Long Island suburb conspire to kill the town slut. They destroy her house. Here, JILL, the victim, in her late twenties, has returned as a ghost and describes to her lover how it felt.

SCENE: Jill's house.

TIME: The present.

JILL's house. After lovemaking. BILL and JILL are in each other's arms, crushed between belongings.

JILL: Being bulldozed sure sobers a girl up fast. I hadn't seen anything like it since I did Windowpane in boarding school. First, when I woke up, the bedroom door had moved to the foot of the bed and was coming closer. Then the sides of the ceiling spread apart and I only had time to squint up at the rising sun before bricks and tiles and baby birds fell in on me. Then the floor buckled beneath my bed and I landed in the living room, my good china dropping on my head and breaking to pieces on my pillow. Then *that* floor fell, and I flew out of bed into the basement, landing face first on the cold concrete. As I flew, I looked up and saw my furniture was following me down—a Saks sofa and a digital sound system, dropping like so much shit—and above it, earlier occupants of the house, a soldier and his wife, screaming and swirling, like they were both just being flushed. The last thing I heard was my smoke alarm going off as, on impact, the foundation cracked beneath my cheek—it just tore in two like a cheap shirt makes a rag—and, twisting like a tornado, my home and I were sucked into the Earth. *(beat)* You didn't see any of that on TV.

GOODNIGHT DESDEMONA (GOOD MORNING, JULIET) by Ann-Marie MacDonald

CONSTANCE LEDBETTER, a woebegone academic in her twenties, has a theory: two of Shakespeare's tragedies, *Othello* and *Romeo and Juliet*, are based on earlier plays by an unknown author. Connie magically falls into the plays as a bonafide character. She is able to straighten them out but not without consequences to herself.

She has just met Desdemona who is grateful that Constance had exposed Iago's perfidy to Othello. Desdemona is going off to help her husband fight the Turks and commands Connie to fight.

SCENE: Venice, Italy.

TIME: During the action of *Othello*.

CONSTANCE:
(Another cannon blast)
                              Omigod!
Oh Constance, don't be scared, it's just a play,
and Desdemona will be looking after you.
Desdemona! I am verging on
the greatest academic breakthrough of
the twentieth century!
I merely must determine authorship.
But have I permanently changed the text?
—You're floundering in the waters of a flood;
the Mona Lisa and a babe float by.
Which one of these two treasures do you save?
I've saved the baby, and let the Mona drown—
Or did the Author know that I'd be coming here,
and leave a part for me to play? How am I cast?
As cast-away to start, but what's my role?

I entered, deus ex machina,
and Desdemona will not die,
because I dropped in from the sky…
Does that make this a comedy?
And does it prove my thesis true?
In that case, I've preempted the Wise Fool!
He must be here somewhere—I'll track him down
and reinstate him in the text,
and then I'll know who wrote this travesty,
since every scholar worth her salt agrees,
the Fool, is the mouthpiece of the Author!
It's all so strange…What's even stranger though—
*(she counts the beat of her speech by tapping each of the five fingers of
    one hand onto the palm of the other, in time with her words)*
I speak in blank verse like the characters:
unrhymed iambical pentameter.
It seems to come quite nat'rally to me.
I feel so eloquent and…*(making up the missing beats)* eloquent.
My god. Perhaps I'm on an acid trip.
What if some heartless student spiked my beer?!
(stops counting) Nonsense. This is my head, this is my
pen, this is *Othello*, Act III Scene iii.
(Sounds of the fray within)
[DESDEMONA *(within)*: Constance, the fray!]
                                    Desdemon, I obey!

GOODNIGHT DESDEMONA (GOOD MORNING, JULIET) by
Ann-Marie MacDonald

**CONSTANCE LEDBETTER, a woebegone academic in her twenties, has
a theory: two of Shakespeare's tragedies, *Othello* and *Romeo and Juliet*,
are based on earlier plays by an unknown author. Connie magically falls
into the plays as a bonafide character. She is able to straighten them out
but not without consequences to herself.**

**Transported into *Romeo and Juliet*, Connie—dressed in long johns—is
mistaken for a man by Mercutio, Tybalt, and Romeo. They are deeply**

grateful that Connie has revealed the marriage of Romeo and Juliet and prevented the swordfight leading to Tybalt's death. They invite her to go to the baths with them for some roughhouse.

SCENE: Verona, Italy.

TIME: During the action of *Romeo and Juliet*.

CONSTANCE: No, wait! I can't! I had a bath today.
(struggling down)
What's more, I've got a lot of things to do;
I have to buy a lute, a sword, some hose,
and teach a class or two before it's noon,
in time to see a man about a horse.
Thank God they think that I'm a man. *(to God)* Thank you. O thank
    you.
How long can I avoid their locker room?
Those guys remind me of the Stratford shows I've seen,
where each production has a Roman bath:
the scene might be a conference of state,
but steam will rise and billow from the wings,
while full-grown men in Velcro loin-cloths speak,
while snapping towels at each other.
Why is it Juliet's scenes with her Nurse
are never in a sauna. Or *King Lear*:
imagine Goneril and Regan, steaming
as they plot the downfall of their Dad,
while tearing hot wax from each other's legs;
Ophelia, drowning in a whirlpool full
of naked women. Portia, pumping iron—
[*(A woman screams within. Male laughter)*]
(verge of tears) I want to go home.
I want to see my cats. I want to read
Jane Eyre again and never leave the house.
Where's the Fool? Where's the damn Fool?!
How come I end up doing all his work?
I should have waited in the wings
for him to leap on stage and stop the fight,

63

and then I could have pinned him down
and forced him to reveal the Author's name!
The Author—who must know my true identity. The Author! who—I
    have to pee...
There must be a convent around here somewhere.

GROUNDHOG by Elizabeth Swados

**A musical portrait of a sister and brother, GILA, about thirty, and
Groundhog. He is a street person fighting New York City's attempts to
commit him to Bellevue. His fight with bureaucracy has earned him a lot
of attention and made him a folk hero. But Gila worries because she
knows he really is mentally ill.**

SCENE: Gila's apartment.

TIME: The present.

GILA *(half sung)*: Someone is trying to get me to commit a crime,
or jump out a window. Or commit myself to Bellevue in Groundhog's
place. It's a nasty practical joke and I'm falling for it. Hard.

I mean he's everywhere right now. He's on the Nightly News, the
talk shows, radio call-in shows, newspapers, magazine covers, public
service announcements, and print ads. It was enough that his voice
never left my head. Now his face swirls around me like the mirrors in
a funhouse.

I just don't get it. Doesn't anyone see who he *really* is? Or is it
possible I was wrong all these years? Could he have recovered? Is
there new medication I don't know about? Did he need to be a hero to
become sane? Maybe it's *me* who brought out the worst in him. I'd
really like to kill him. I miss him when he's witty like this. My
brother's mind is quick. But just wait till he turns. He's like a kid, isn't
he? Now he's playing a game called political action. He could possibly
mean what he says. Maybe he believes himself. They're using him.
Don't they seem to care about his well-being? He's no doubt using
them. It's like the Emperor's New Clothes. Nobody sees the real truth.
Not that I claim to know the absolute truth myself. Oh God I'm so

64

obsessed. Don't worry, they'll call me when it all falls apart. This time I hope it doesn't. Or do I? Maybe I need him to fail. That's a little harsh. Shut up, Gila. Shut up. I'd vowed I'd be liberated from Groundhog. Now that I'm without him, I've never been more attached. His reemergence in my life is stifling. But it's oddly *comforting* to know where he is for a change. However, none of the old dread has disappeared. I think I do know the Groundhog no one wants to know. And that's why I'm banished. Fuck this. I'm going out.

HIDE THE BRIDE by Sari Bodi

GAYLA, in her twenties or thirties, is a young bride who left her groom at the altar when her Latin lover, Amelio, arrived at the church. To escape Amelio and her torrid past with him, she runs away to a nearby suburban home where she re-establishes marital relations with her husband, Parker. But Amelio has tracked her down.

SCENE: A suburban home.

TIME: The present.

GAYLA: How dare you follow me here, Amelio. Can't you see how well-suited I am to married life? Parker and I were just having our first breakfast together as man and wife where we prioritized our long-range marital goals. No! Do not take that dress out of your pack. You are trying to remind me of a steamy hot summer night. You are on the dance floor. Every woman is staring at you in your clinging black pants and matching eyepatch. You are showing me the cha-cha-cha, and I am covered in red roses. You already ruined my wedding with that dress. It was going to be a perfect day, too. The normally one-word Parker had finally agreed to say "I do" instead of "Acceptance." Oh, and when the bridesmaids arrived, each looked more exquisite than the next in those darling lime green dresses (It's Parker's favorite color.) All posing together in front of the aged-oak church doors, smiling selflessly into the camera. And when the church doors swung open, and we heard Lohengrin's wedding march boom out of the biggest pipe organ ever seen in a community of moderate size, and every woman reached for her purse-sized packet of wedding tissue, I thought to myself, this is all for me. Today, I'm Scarlett O'Hara. I'm the Queen of England. I'm Cleopatra before she was killed by the snake. I felt like there were a hundred angels flying overhead singing the Hallelujah chorus in angelic harmony. And I floated down the aisle as if my feet were being cushioned by millions and millions of miniature marshmallows, drawing well-deserved gasps from all those Parker P. Parkers from Old Lyme, Connecticut. And then, when I reached Parker, he said to me in a voice choked with hitherto-unreleased male emotion, "Fulfillment." But then, just as I was about to triumphantly face the congregation in what would have undeniably been the best moment of my entire existence on this unexplainable earth, you, you step out from behind the minister who has known me since I was an innocent eight years old, and you wickedly wave that horrible, that horrible...dress rojo. Didn't you see that as soon as you waved my red dress, I ran down that aisle as fast as my legs encased in antique wedding gown would carry me? There weren't miniature marshmallows under my feet anymore. There were hot coals. My fire was back. Oh, give me that damn dress rojo. Are my desires still in it?

THE INNOCENTS CRUSADE by Keith Reddin

Bill is sixteen and conceives the idea of leading a Children's Crusade for truth and idealism to the Holy Land. He changes his name to Stephen like the boy leader in the middle ages and picks up young converts on the way. LAURA, one of the teenage disciples, explains the cause to Bill's—or Stephen's—skeptical father:

SCENE: A motel room.

TIME: The present.

LAURA: But it's happening, Mr. Sherman. Something is happening. Something started and now it's taking its course and people will hear about it and will want to know more and when they know more they will become excited and once they're excited they'll tell more people and more and it will grow and we'll march and we'll start convoys and wagon trains and armadas and modern pilgrims will meet in roadside restaurants like this and tell stories and somebody will write them down and they'll be like *Canterbury Tales* for today and there'll be a story about you and you and me, "Laura's Story" or the "Waitress' Tale," like that and people will read about what we do or see us on television and want to join us, and some won't but others will and we'll keep moving, we'll be going forward and Stephen, your son, is the start of that. And there'll be stories about him, about me and him meeting, and then Evan joining us and me talking here, right now, there will be a story about that, and people will repeat what I'm saying right now, right this moment so even if what I'm saying doesn't sound all that important now at some other time it will.

THE INNOCENTS CRUSADE by Keith Reddin

Bill Sherman, sixteen, makes the rounds with his parents of college admissions offices. He conceives the idea of leading a Children's Crusade for truth and idealism to the Holy Land. MS. CABOT, in her thirties, the admissions officer, reveals her own earlier crusade for existential meaning.

SCENE: An Ivy League campus.

TIME: The present.

MS. CABOT: Bill, when I was your age, that was...well, I'm not going to tell you how long ago that was, but it was more than a few years, I was pretty much like you. I didn't have any answers. Oh, I knew I wanted to do something to make the world a better place, but I wasn't clear what I, as an individual could do. I wandered around from place to place and menial job to menial, job until I became a very high priced call girl. I was one of the most expensive prostitutes in an exclusive escort service that catered to heads of states and incredibly wealthy businessmen. Once in a while, I would pleasure well-known movie stars or athletes. I would do anything if the price was right, and it always was. One time I even...well, I won't go into all that now, but like I said, nothing was beyond me. Then one day a man came to me and wanted to sleep with me and I asked his name because he looked very familiar to me and do you know who that man was? No, Bill. He was my father. My father who didn't know who I was, but I asked him some questions and he told me he lost his little girl in a plane crash. But of *course* that wasn't true, and I slept with him, but seeing him I realized what my life had become; that I had to change my life, and I did. I took my savings, which were quite substantial, and I went back to school and I majored in education and I taught for a while and then I came here. And now you and I are talking. I'm saying it was a pleasure spending this time with you and I wish you luck on whatever college you end up attending and don't worry, it's not the end of the world if you don't get accepted here, because I think you're a very bright young man and obviously want to do big things. And I think, if you have a Crusade you should follow that Crusade wherever it takes you. Because a good Crusade comes along only every thousand years or so and when they do you got to jump on it before it moves on. I'd consider joining your Crusade except I have tenure here and we also have an excellent health plan which is rare. I wish I could be on the road again, but…Listen, if the Crusade thing pans out, drop me a line, would you? Don't let any one tell you differently, Bill, we live in very exciting times.

JOINED AT THE HEAD by Catherine Butterfield

Maggie Mulroney is a sucessful novelist whose books are popular with women. She has returned to her hometown near Boston to autograph her latest novel, *Joined at the Head*, a tale of father and daughter. She meets her old high school boyfriend, Jim, who has married a woman named MAGGY, in her thirties, who is dying of cancer. Maggy and Maggie become friends. Here Maggy recalls her thoughts about Maggie in high school and how she met Jim.

SCENE: A Boston apartment.

TIME: The present.

MAGGY: Jim and I met at a Fourth of July parade, did he tell you that? He was standing there watching the floats, and I kind of sidled over and stood next to him. I remembered him from school. In fact, I remembered him as your boyfriend. It was surprising to see him standing there by himself all those years later, looking sort of lost and lonely. I just assumed he'd married you and gone off to become a big shot somewhere—you know, Brown Book Award and all. Anyway, there I stook next to Jim looking at the parade, feeling kind of stupid, and here's what I thought: "if I were Maggie Mulroney right now, what would I say?" And at that moment a float went by with Gina Lazlo on it. She was looking a little the worse for wear—to tell you the truth she kind of peaked in the 12th grade. She was all dolled up as some kind of overweight sex goddess on a float that said Bigelow Pontiac—she married Robbie Bigelow, did you know that? So here she is on Robbie's float waving a wand, you really had to be there to appreciate the full impact, and I said, "Living proof. You drive 'em off the lot, and they lose their value instantly." And he looked at me like I'd just arrived on the planet, one of those "what have we here?" looks, you know? And I felt like a million dollars. Suddenly, with my new personality, I felt so free and liberated. It was great. But after awhile I started to worry. I said to myself, "This isn't really you. Who is it?" And of course I knew the answer right away. It was you. I was so in awe of you back in school, Maggie. You seemed absolutely ferocious. I loved your optimism, your sense that anything was possible. And most of all, I loved your anger, because that was one thing I just couldn't express myself. My mother was an alcoholic. Even conscious, she was never what you would call presentable. I spent all my time trying to fool everybody, convince them we were a normal family. And for the most part, I managed to pull it off—But God! I was so angry underneath. At my mother, for taking away my childhood. But mostly at myself, for being such a "good girl," for letting everybody push me around. You don't know how much I wanted to go to that demonstration in Boston with all of you and scream at the top of my lungs, "This is wrong! This is wrong! This is—" (*Her face contorts*) Where's that—? (*She finds her bowl and dry heaves into it*) Sorry about that. Thought I was going to lose it for a minute.

LAST CALL FOREVER by Leonard Melfi

Five smalltown young people encounter each other for the first time and face the same problem—the death of a loved one. Their youth has left them unprepared for their loss.

MELLOW LEGS, a pretty blonde in her early twenties, has led a privileged life. She explains how this has sheltered her from reality.

SCENE: A bar in upstate New York.

TIME: The present. Two-something in the morning.

MELLOW: Oh, my, my! You did that on the night of the same day as your mother's funeral?! Oh, my, my! It's so ironic...because I went to a funeral this morning. That's why I'm so drunk right now. This bartender kept feeding me a drink called Slippery Nipples. It's a shot-glass almost filled with San Buca, and then, on the top of it is poured Bailey's Irish Cream. And it never mingles with the San Buca...the Irish Cream just stays on the top of the shot-glass...The Bailey's and the San Buca never mix together, not until you down the whole shot in one nice slow gulp...and then you get the sensation, and that's when you realize why it's called a Slippery Nipple. *(A pause.)* You'd never think I was still a virgin, would you all, now? Especially since the way I've been talking. But let me tell you all something?! I know everything about sex, even if I really haven't experienced it completely yet! My nickname is Mellow Legs because I've got just that: a pair of nice mellow legs! Look! *(She shows them.)* And I just know that none of you believe I'm a virgin because of the way I look, because I know that I look pretty goddam good, let me tell you! But that's the way it is. My mother and my father raised me like an ornamental doll, and then they got divorced, and she moved to West Palm Beach, and he lives in London, and I live with my rich aunt and uncle on Riverside Drive, and I never have to worry about anything. *(A pause.)* This is the first time I've really ever been out like this, at this hour, and all by myself, my poor little self! Except don't get me wrong: I'm not feeling sorry for myself. *(A pause.)* By the way, sir...you who had such a fantastic romantic escapade in the back of a Greyhound bus after your mother's funeral...what's your name?

LAST CALL FOREVER by Leonard Melfi

Five smalltown young people encounter each other for the first time and face the same problem—the death of a loved one. Their youth has left them unprepared for their loss.

MELLOW LEGS, a pretty blonde in her early twenties, has led a privileged life. This has sheltered her from reality, causing her to live a life of fantasies, like this one about her friend Dr. Maze.

SCENE: A bar in upstate New York.

TIME: The present. Two-something in the morning.

MELLOW: It's not civilized! "Last Call"..."Last Call"..."Last Call"...! I was never so disappointed in my whole life when I found out what it actually meant! I mean I just simply spent the worst day of my life today! I went to my shrink's funeral this morning. Yes, my shrink's sad little funeral right here in the middle of town. Oh, did I ever love him...he was the best in the city...as far as I'm concerned: the best doctor-shrink anywhere! You couldn't top Dr. Maze! What a dream he was! I'd been going to him for over five years now. Mommy and Daddy took care of the bills from Dr. Maze. I never had to worry about anything. He was so handsome. A real dream-of-a-guy. I used to wish and pray that he'd get a divorce, but it never happened. He died of a sudden heart attack, without any warning. When I saw him lying there in his coffin in his light blue suit, and his light blue shirt, and his cream-colored necktie, well, I almost just wanted to jump in there with him, right on top of him, and then whisper into his right ear, whisper to him to move over so that I could be lying side-by-side instead, like in some hotel room on our honeymoon, maybe in the middle of Europe somewhere. I went to school in Florence, Italy for awhile. Maybe in Florence: that would be a lovely place for our honeymoon together, don't you think? Oh, God, I wish I had had the nerve to jump on top of him for a second or two, not caring what people would think! But I didn't...I held back as usual...just like my whole life, always holding

71

back! *(A pause.)* I couldn't cry when I first saw him lying there in his gleaming silver coffin. I didn't cry at the funeral either. The only time I cried was when I first read about his death in the obituaries in the newspapers. I guess the reason I haven't cried since is because I must be in a state of shock or I don't believe it, or both. *(A pause.)* Do you know what I went and did? *(Whispering now.)* Well, I'll tell you people, but please don't tell anyone else. You've got to keep it a secret, otherwise, if it gets around, they'll lock me up in a mental ward for good and throw away the key, too! I slipped a little box of condoms inside of Dr. Mark Maze's coffin, right underneath where his right elbow was, sort of pushing the little box of condoms down in the yellow satin of the coffin without anybody even noticing...!

I thought that Dr. Maze would get the biggest kick out of it. He had an absolutely wonderful sense of humor. He knew exactly how to deal with me, no matter what. Right now, I can just hear him. "Mellow Legs," he would say to me. "Why did you go and do that?" "Why did I go and do what, Dr. Maze?" I would say back to him very innocent-like. "Why did you slip that little box of condoms inside of my coffin with me, Mellow Legs?" he would say back to me. "Well, now, Dr. Maze," I would say back to him, batting my eyelashes every so often. "I believe in life after death, and, well, now that you're gone, who knows what's going to happen to me...except that I may have to join you...and, well, in this day and age, during these really screwed-up times, we just simply have to play it safe, whether we're dead or alive, Dr. Maze!" *(A pause.)* Now this is really a secret! Please, everybody?! Well, there were a number of times when Dr. Maze looked like he was going to be the one who would finally end my virgin state of being. It was always my fault that it didn't happen, I'm now very sad and sorry to say. But his sense of humor, his deep, sexy laugh...they were enough for me at that time. Once, he asked me what I was going to have engraved on my tombstone. I thought for a second or two, and then I said to him: "It'll say: 'Who said you can't take it with you?'" Well, he just laughed and laughed...he couldn't stop his laughing for the rest of the day, or any time he ever thought of it after that. *(A pause.)* I loved him! I...loved...him! *(A pause.)* I love him more right now than I ever did when he was alive and well and kicking around all over the place! *(A pause.)* I guess I'll be suffering now for the rest of my life.

LIFE DURING WARTIME by Keith Reddin

GALE, a woman in her thirties, has been killed in a burglary. She had a boyfriend named Tommy. Here, she appears as a ghost and tells us of her thwarted ambitions and hopes.

SCENE: The home of Gale and her son.

TIME: The present.

GALE: I wanted to do so much with life. I wanted to paint and take pictures and play the piano. I wanted my son Howard to be a doctor or a pilot or a film director. None of those things happened. Instead I sold real estate for Century Twenty-One.

There was a poem I loved. It went:

anyone lived in a pretty how town
with up so floating many bells down
spring summer autumn winter
he sang his didn't he danced his did

Women and men (both little and small)
cared for anyone not at all
they sowed their isn't
they reaped their same
sun moon stars rain

when by now and tree by leaf
she laughed his joy she cried his grief
bid by snow and stir by still
anyones any was all to her

I wish somebody would write a poem about me. A poem that people would read hundreds of years from now. Maybe my life would make a good poem, I don't know.

Tommy's not a poet, so there's not much chance he'd write one,

73

but he always surprised me.

I'd watch him talking—and I thought was I ever that young? Was I ever that alive and I thought yes I am. I am that alive when I'm in love and I'm loved back and the kitchen floor is wonderful, lying in his arms on the kitchen floor, I was very alive.

And we chose to be on that floor. And maybe we sinned but we chose to sin. And I'd do it again, and there is nothing unpure about that. Think about it.

LIPS TOGETHER TEETH APART by Terrence McNally

Sam Truman, his wife Sally, his sister CHLOE, and Chloe's husband John—all in their late thirties—are spending the July 4th weekend at the Long Island beach house which belonged to Sally's brother, who died of AIDS.

Chloe, a gregarious type, treats everyone to details of their community theater production of *Guys and Dolls*. She also is a compulsive organizer; you either like her vivacity or hate her not minding her own business. At various times, all the characters are brought down by her grim determination to stay "up."

Here, she's been ordered by her dour husband, John, to stay quiet and "keep a total ban on all sounds emanating from your throat for the next six hours."

With wounded dignity, she speaks to them all.

SCENE: A beach house on Long Island.

TIME: The present.

CHLOE: I'll get the second act down pat. I think you should know something about me. All of you. I think it is precisely the small things I run on about and that seem to annoy you so—the little day-to-day details, the nuances—that give our lives some zip and some meaning. I care about cooking the burgers so each of you get exactly what you ask for. I worry about who's driving the children's car pool that particular week. I notice what's going on around me, every detail. I don't miss a thing. I've got all your numbers. I talk too much, probably because it's too horrible to think about what's really going on. You should try it, Miss Broody-Woody, Miss Highfalutin! You think you're so superior. Well, maybe you are. But to whom? Me? Honey, just about anyone is superior to me. You're going to have to do a lot better than that if you want to keep that attitude up. I'll try to think of something lofty to say at dinner. *(She starts to go to her room, then turns back.)* You know, I'm not mad at any of you. Really. I think we're all pathetic. Sally, will you clean up? We'll have bugs galore. Pussy Galore! Remember her?

THE LOMAN FAMILY PICNIC by Donald Margulies

DORIS, thirty-eight, is a depressive who fantasizes about leaving her husband Herbie, an appliance fixtures salesman. That's okay, since he fantasizes about leaving her too. Their son Mitchell is writing a musical version of *Death of a Salesman* called *Willy!* and their other son, Stewie, is about to have a Bar Mitzvah they can't afford.

Doris wears a housecoat over her pajamas (she's too depressed to get up) and sits on the sofa with her wedding dress in her lap. She is cutting it to shreds with a pair of scissors.

SCENE: A highrise apartment in Coney Island.

TIME: Around 1965.

DORIS *(To us.)*: On the day I was married the world showed every sign of coming to an end. It rained—no, poured. Thunder. Cracks of lightning. Big Pearl S. Buck tidal waves. You get the picture. Did I turn back? Did I cancel? Did I say never mind, no thank you? A good omen, my mother told me. There had never been such a terrifying convergence of weather post-Noah; a good omen. Hail, did I mention hail? Like my mother's matzo balls falling from the sky shouting *Don't! Don't!* each time a knaidel smacked the roof of the rented limo. A better omen still, my mother said, hail. What about sunshine, Momma?, I asked, what about a sunny wedding day? Also a good omen, my mother said. *(A beat.)* I began to distrust her. *(A beat.)* Two seconds in my wedding dress: splattered with mud. I should've known. Look at this: ruined. From day one. *(Points to various stains.)* Mud, rain, hail, locusts, boredom, moraine... *(Looking directly at us.)* I love the way my life has turned out. I have two wonderful boys. Mitchell is my baby. He's eleven. And Stewie is gonna be bar mitzvahed next Saturday at ten in the morning, to be followed by a gala affair starring me. What boys I have! I'm very lucky, knock on formica. Smart?! Mitchell has a reading level, goes off the charts. So smart are my boys. Their father is not at all threatened by how smart they are. They aren't showoffs. I don't like showoffs. I raised my boys to stand out but not too much, you know?, otherwise people won't like you anymore. Look what happened to the Jews in Europe. Better you should have friends and be popular, than be showy and alone. My Aunt Marsha may she rest in peace taught me that. She was very popular. *(A beat. Refers to the wedding dress.)* Last night was my wedding anniversary. Eighteen years. Herbie had to work, what else is new. I love the way my life has turned out. Did I say that already? On the day I was married the world showed every sign of coming to an end...

LOOSE KNIT by Theresa Rebeck

Three members of a knitting club find themselves having dates with the same man. Miles is arrogant, cold, and rich. He owns a couple of very ritzy cars. MARGIE, about thirty, meets Miles for their date.

SCENE: A sushi restaurant.

TIME: The present.

MARGIE: *(Abashed)* Well. I do think it's nice to have beautiful things. In your life. I wish I had beautiful things in my life. I wish I had your car in my life. I mean, I'm glad it's in my life. It's in my life tonight, anyway, and I find that really just—wonderful. And I find you fascinating, but I also want to tell you to fuck off. Do you know what I mean? I mean, I don't really want to tell you to fuck off, really what I want to do is have sex in the back seat of that amazing car, but frankly, I don't know, I'm really just so stunned by all this, stunned and repulsed you know? The thought of kissing you makes my blood run cold but on the other hand, I'm really hoping that you'll pick me. Pick me, Miles. Pick me. Let's not waste time. That's why I signed up for that stupid dating service, because I didn't want to waste any more time, I don't have any more time to waste, but women aren't supposed to do that sort of thing, we don't choose, do we, you guys are the ones who do the choosing. Well, sometimes we FORGET THAT, ALL RIGHT? I wish I would shut up; I really do but I just don't think that's going to happen. What is the matter with me? Why can't I do this? I'm really sorry. It's just, you know—you can't just be like this, but you are, and I—I want you. I want to fuck you in the back seat of that car. You make me sick.

LOST IN YONKERS by Neil Simon

BELLA, a retarded woman in her mid-thirties, lives with her mother, Grandma Kurnitz, a German-accented tyrant. Bella has found a man whom she wants to marry. Incredulous, Grandma Kurnitz asks what else this man could want from her but her money.

SCENE: A house in Yonkers, New York, that sits above Kurnitz's Kandy store.

TIME: 1942.

BELLA: Me! He wants *me!* He wants to marry me! *(She starts to cry)* I want to marry *him*...I want to have his children...I want my own babies. [LOUIE *(Sits back)*: Jesus Christ! GRANDMA *(Shocked at this)*: Dot's enough!...I don't vant to hear dis anymore!] You think I can't have healthy babies, Momma? Well, I can...I'm as strong as an ox. I've worked in that store and taken care of you by myself since I'm twelve years old, that's how strong I am...Like *steel,* Momma. Isn't that how we're supposed to be?...But my babies won't die because I'll love them and take care of them...And they won't get sick like me or Gert or be weak like Eddie and Louie...My babies will be happier than we were because I'll teach them to be happy...Not to grow up and run away or never visit when they're older or not be able to breathe because they're so frightened...and never, *ever* to make them spend their lives rubbing my back and my legs because you never had anyone around who loved you enough to want to touch you because you made it so clear you never wanted to be touched with love...Do you know what it's like to touch steel, Momma? It's hard and it's cold and I want to be warm and soft with my children...Let me have my babies, Momma. Because I have to love somebody. I have to love someone who'll love me back before I die...Give me that, Momma, and I promise you, you'll never worry about being alone...Because you'll have us...Me and my husband and my babies...Louie, tell her how wonderful that would be...Gert, wouldn't that make her happy?...Momma?...Please say yes...I need you to say yes...Please? *(It is deathly silent. No one has moved. Finally, GRANDMA gets up slowly, walks to her room, goes in, and quietly closes the door. BELLA looks at the others)* Hold me...Somebody please hold me.

MAGENTA SHIFT by Carol Mack

JANE, an intense-comedic photographer, mid-thirties, has arrived in the subway station to flee a possible pursuer. Cameras hang from her neck and mittens wave, as she shares her angst with subway booth operator Rhea.

SCENE: A subway station.

TIME: The present.

JANE: Listen, first I better tell you the problem. I mean the heart of the problem. O.K.? Did you...did you ever hear of the Magenta Shift? It's what's happening to all our photographs? The problem started with the Kennedy photographs. The color? See when all those photographs aged, the color started to shift. And then the first dominant color was magenta, which is how they named it the Magenta Shift and then...what happens is there's a slow fade. A fade to absolutely nothing! And that's the problem. Everything's fading out!

Soon there'll be no record at all. Of anything!

(Jane sits, overwhelmed with that)

That was only the background. I can only tell this a piece at a time. It's too powerful. So…O.K., about a month ago a woman calls my studio. She says her wedding pictures are turning pink. All the bridesmaids who'd been wearing blue are now wearing magenta. O.K., I say, calm down. Just take them out of your album and put them in the refrigerator. See, she's gotta put them in the refrigerator or else her wedding cake turns magenta, and then slowly the entire party would lose *that* color and fade out like it never even happened! It's guaranteed to keep in cold storage for more than five hundred years. Five. *Hundred.* Years! Get it?

(Intensely)

Don't you get it?! Five hundred years! Who's gonna look in Mrs. Sugarman's refrigerator?! Where is her refrigerator going to BE in five hundred years! That's from Columbus to now! That's from like Descartes to Derrida! At the rate we're going? That refrigerator will be under some lifeless sea. ALL our photographs are turning mooncolor as we talk, and who cares? What *are* photographs but a collection of silver specks! Somebody's got to BE there to decode them!

(Beat)

All those photos are dots. They're all just *moments.* They have absolutely no *meaning* without people to experience them! Oh my God! And how about our books? Disintegrating? *(claps her hands) Now,* this second fifty million words just *went.* It's triage in the stacks. And all those *bindings*! They want to put it all on microfilm, send the books to Greenland and sink them under ice. Kids will grow up and not know what a *page* is! What's left? Frozen books! Who's going to defrost them! Who?

MAGENTA SHIFT by Carol Mack

RHEA, a middle-aged African-American woman of great presence and comedic gifts, is telling her life story to her new friend, Jane.

SCENE: A subway token booth where Rhea works.

TIME: The present, 2 A.M.

79

RHEA: Now you listen. I'm going to tell you bout my pet, Rory. No bigger than a white rat, Rory is. I had one of *them* for a week once. That's when MY story starts. My Boy took it home from school when he was bout eight. I say to the teacher, I say: we already got a lot of these type animal round here. Why stick *this* one in a cage? Why should it get itself served breakfast when the other ones is out in the garbage huntin for themselves?

(She regards JANE a beat)

She say, "This rat is an Albino Rat. This is our Class Rat." Well it was one ugly thing when you got close up. So one mornin while the Boy was gettin milk from the store, I just let it out. And that was the mornin the Boy shows off his potential for what he'd be when he growed up. He sees the cage door open and he knocks me right down and kicks me bloody in the head and the belly, and he was only in third *grade* at that time!...Well, the School Psychologist, she say the Boy tol her his Mama killed the White Rat but *she* knew "such a thing was not possible!" She knew it had to be an "accident" and it was all a matter of "CO-munication" but she didn't see I had iodine all over cause the Boy bit me too and maybe had the rabies from playin with that ALBINO rat!

So. I look at her and I ask does she want to con-tinue this dis-cussion bout co-munication in my cage? Cause I'd be there in the night shift makin my rent so the Boy don't have to eat outta the garbage and get hisself killed like the Class Rat. (she laughs suddenly) That's when she ask me... *(hoots)* "What is your line of work?" WHAT IS YOUR LINE?

(Hoots and her laugh is infectious. JANE joins in helplessly)

They had this T.V. program back then they'd light up under your chin...you remember, no. See they'd get these people who looked like somethin they wasn't. And the job lights under the chin: This guy is a DISHWASHER! An everybody break up cause the guy next to him who LOOK like a dishwasher, he's really a banker. It gave me the idea! *(remembers clearly)* I think I'm gonna say somethin to this Psychologist Lady an see if my light come on. I say: "I am a practicing surgeon by day, and by night I tell fortunes in a glass booth."

(JANE watches RHEA intently as she recognizes wording her smile fades)

(Cool, angry, remembering)

The Psychologist act like she don't hear. Jus writes in her book, says the Boy is disruptin. I figure since she is not impressed by my two fabulous careers, I won't talk no more. Then she asks me direct bout the Boy's Daddy and that's when I decide *she* looks like that Class Rat around the mouth. *(RHEA stops. Pulls herself together and then looks at her nails)* I say, "funny you askin bout the Boy's Daddy, cause I do not know fer sure who that is." NOW she's interested! I say, don't worry cause they tied up my tubes so the Boy won't ever have no "Sibling Rivalry"....*(bitter)* I could sound just like that fool if I wanted.

SO. After the Rat there's LOTS of visitors. I always give em a cup of coffee and keep the kitchen real clean, but soon the Boy stop goin to school...

I'm tellin you about Rory.

I'm tellin you bout when they come to visit. See I used to fool them with little things like I had this one big bar of Visitor Soap. When they came I put it out on top of the sink and there it sit. The letters say I-V-O-R-Y, cut deep into the soap and not rubbed down none so you could see from across the room like this sign's blinkin: I-Vory, I-Vory, like saying this lady is a *neat* lady with a *clean* sink and no scum on her soap bar! Yeah. So you can't take her son away from her...

(Looks hard at JANE)

Little thing like that keep you outta trouble a *long* time. But the joke's on me...

MARVIN'S ROOM by Scott McPherson

In this black comedy, Bessie takes care of her father, Marvin, after he has a stroke. When Bessie develops leukemia, her sister LEE and Lee's son Hank come to Florida from Ohio to see if they can provide bone marrow to save her.

Lee is a nervous woman, a smoker, a part-time beautician. Hank, a disturbed boy of seventeen who burned down his family's house, has just come from a mental institution. He cannot remember his

father, who Lee threw out years ago.

The family visits Disney World, where Hank is by turns taciturn and belligerent. Finally, Lee has enough.

SCENE: Disney World in Florida. On a bench.

TIME: The present.

Do you want to know the truth about your dad? I was just pregnant with Charlie. I was out late one day doing the Christmas shopping. Buying toys. So your dad was taking care of you. I came home and I hear you up in the bath. I come in without knocking and your dad is up on his knees, leaning his thick body over the tub and with one hand on your throat he is holding you under the water. Do you hear me? He was holding you under the water. I threw myself at him, Christmas presents I was carrying jammed between us. I broke one of his ribs and it pierced his lung. He fell back between the toilet and sink. Wheezing. You pop out of the water like a balloon, gasping for breath. The two of you wheezing and gasping. I grab you out of the tub and we leave the house, you naked and wet, we go out into the snow.

(*Pause*)

I visit your dad in the hospital. He says he was just trying to stop you from crying. His eyes are wet. He can't look at me. It will never happen again. I say no, it won't, because he is never seeing you again. He is never seeing me. I will not move on this. I will not budge.

(*Pause*)

Do you know how much I loved him? If I had come home 5 minutes later and found you dead in the tub, I think I may have stayed with him, somehow. I think I may have. I have room for all sorts of things inside of me. But you weren't dead, thank God, and you are for me to take care of. So I did what I had to do.

(*Pause*)

My feelings for you. Hank, are like a big bowl of fish hooks. I can't just pick them up one at a time. I pick up one, they all come. So I tend to leave them alone.

THE MOONSHOT TAPE by Lanford Wilson

DIANE, at thirty-two, is a hard-drinking, serious-smoking writer who has already achieved fame.

She has come back to her home town to move her mother into a nursing home. She reads from a list of typed questions from her high school newspaper for which she has agreed to do an interview.

SCENE: A room at the Ozark Cabins Motel in Mountain Grove, Mississippi.

TIME: A recent spring. Late on a drizzling afternoon.

DIANE: *(She looks at the list.)* "Where do you get your ideas for stories?" *(She sighs, then thinks seriously.)* Well, why not? To begin with most of my critics would have you believe I've never *had* an idea for a story. And, you know, for all I know or care they're right. "Where do I get"...I'm gonna try to answer this truthfully. I've lied to dozens of interviewers about it. A lot of the time they're flat-out portraits of people I know; things in their lives they've been foolish enough to tell me or I've witnessed or surmised. Then I swear it isn't them, how could they think I'd do that? Or, you know, sometimes it's just raw speculation. You see someone, you start making up a story about them. There's a little old woman, probably lives with fifty cats. That guy is a wife beater. Someone on the subway, it's a game, you know, I've always done it. Like the song: *(Singing conversationally.)* "Laughing on the bus, playing games with the strangers. You said the man in the gabardine suit was a spy. I said, 'Be careful, his bow tie is really a camera...'" It makes them less of a stranger. Or at least it's easier than the trouble it would take to meet them. It's a good exercise to get the imagination going. And sometimes it ends with a story. Or, you know, sometimes—well, it's *always,* unfortunately, just yourself you're writing about, but sometimes they're *blatantly* autobiographical My side of the story, that's always fun. Never underestimate the power and excitement of revenge. *(Without a beat she breaks off)* What in the hell is Edith taking so much—probably dishing me to filth. In that superior Christian tone. She's what? Holy

83

Roller, whatever it is, there's a name for it. No lipstick, no movies. Probably married him just so she'd have a legitimate excuse not to read my work. Fiction, good God forbid, the devil's door; and salacious fiction at that. They don't know the half of it. I could curl her toes good but what's the point? Mom married Edith's dad when Edith was about two, I was eleven. Tom, Edith's dad, was a case. Well, actually he was only about three six-packs. And half a fifth of J.W. Dant. The smell still turns my gut. It didn't keep me from drinking, but it kept me from drinking J.W. Dant. "Where do I get my ideas?" Sometimes I start writing something, it turns into a piece that's been kicking me around forever; and I think, oh, good, I'm finally doing that. Then I'll go months with nothing. One thing I haven't done, at least in years, is sit in front of a blank sheet of paper—or now a blank PC screen—and force myself to write. "Now is the time for all good women to come to the aid of their party." If they had one. I always wait till I'm—well, I started to say inspired, that's a little sweeping—at least until I have someone or some incident or some place or some event in mind. Like if you weren't here now I might be writing a story about a woman coming home to help her mother move into a Nursing Home. Or just coming back for a visit and seeing the town or someone from school, or any of the things coming back home does to you. Being invaded by those memories, those times, those voices, the pictures. The moonshot, watching it on TV, imagining that silence, that airlessness, weightlessness, kicking up that dust that hadn't been kicked up before and doesn't settle immediately because of the weak gravity. That barren place. Or graduation; *that* barren place. Or being interviewed by a terminally shy young high school reporter and filling her tape with maundering stories of the first moonshot.—And the various lies you tell of your history to protect the guilty. But probably coming back to this particular town I'd just be getting drunk so don't feel you're usurping my time; no other interviewer has. I'd more likely be watching TV. We get channels two, seven and almost ten. So. *(She looks at the paper again, tired of this, exasperated, almost pissed.)* "How much of an influence has Mountain Grove been on your writing comma your life?" Buckets. Whole bucketsful. *(Pause.)* I'm sorry. You've caught me at low ebb, or a bad time. I have all these feelings, guilt-trips, ghosts, bombarding me here. How much of an influence has Mountain Grove been? Never underestimate that either, and in

84

little ways. The first boyfriend I had at B.U.—for all our free love talk in high school, I'd managed to remain a virgin, squirming out from under basketball players in the back seats of Camaros. I can't imagine *why*. What kind of morality is that? It's all right to be felt up till you're literally raw, French-kiss all night, jerk 'em off even, if that's what it takes, but preserve the integrity of your hymen at all costs. Oh, lord. For all the flaws in our design, and with Mother lately I'm beginning to realize the human body is not nearly the miracle it seems when you're eighteen, but as for the hymen: *Think* of the sweeping changes it would make in the history of Man if Woman had never been designed with that particular membrane. Anyway, I had this boyfriend for about a month. We went on a picnic, walking through the woods. The poor guy had never been in the country before in his life. I'm stomping through the underbrush, I look back and this bastard is getting slapped in the face with every sapling in the forest. He had no idea how to walk in the woods. So I lost some respect for him in that hidden place where we judge men, and didn't see him much after that. I'd say over by the oak tree and he'd say, which one is that. No. I couldn't seriously consider someone who can't tell a birch from a beech. I was thankful that he took my virginity with him, but that was about it. And introducing me to Swinburne which was important to me then. And tells you quite a bit about both of us.

THE MOONSHOT TAPE by Lanford Wilson

DIANE, at thirty-two, is a hard-drinking, serious-smoking writer who has already achieved fame.

She has come back to her home town to move her mother into a nursing home. A childhood victim of her stepfather Tom's sexual abuse, Diane now has the opportunity for revenge.

SCENE: A room at the Ozark Cabins Motel in Mountain Grove, Mississippi.

TIME: A recent spring. Late on a drizzling afternoon.

DIANE: So I came back here, for our fifth high school reunion,

85

contrived to get everyone but Tom out of the house one Sunday afternoon. Tom was very respectful. I was important, of course, and an adult now. And Tom had found God. So I showed him how the police tied us up to take us off to jail—they hadn't actually, and as a matter of fact, I was never in jail, but it comes in handy from time to time to be able to tell a story. Which he told me later was just lying and getting away with it. So there he was, with his feet belted together and his hands tied behind his back, lying on the living room floor. I wish you could have seen it gradually...dawn on him that he was helpless... *(Pause. She lights a cigarette. Maybe she pours a couple of fingers of vodka and has a belt as well.)* Never underestimate the power and excitement of revenge. *(Beat.)* I wandered into the kitchen, got myself a soda from the fridge. Tom started calling, "Diane? Where'd you go, honey? Diane, this ain't funny, sweetheart." I looked around the kitchen, some of the drawers. I hadn't realized, lord above, Mom had a regular slaughterhouse in her knife drawer. Mallets and cleavers and a collection of butcher knives that was absolutely *sobering.* But I selected the weapon of my trade—an indelible—permanent ink felt tip pen that mom used to mark packages of meat for the locker plant or deep freeze and I went back into the room with Tom. He was thinking very fast, but he didn't say anything. So I sat down beside him on the floor and very slowly started unbuttoning his shirt and pants, with him starting to say now, "Oh, don't do that, Diane, Honey, I'm gonna tell your mother," if you can believe it. I went back into the kitchen, got the scissors, scared him to death, but only to cut his clothes off him, around the rope and my belt and his belt that I had hog-tied him with. Which *really* pissed him off—his Sunday suit pants and good new Arrow shirt. I just said, "Tom, don't tell me you've forgot all our nights together." I was stroking his stomach and his dick. You've never seen anyone struggle so hard not to get an erection. I just said, "You're coming into my room, it's dark and quiet and smells like Evening in Paris body powder. You pull the covers down off my perky little breasts." He's yelling, "I don't know what you're talking about, you just dreamed that." I said, "Why, Daddy, that's every little girl's dream—in the minds of men." And "Oh, there, finally, is that big ol' fat stubby hard dick with the pointy head I been lookin' for." He's trying to roll over so I straddled him. He's saying, "Don't do nothin', whatta you doin'?" I told him, "Now, Tom, Peepin' Tom, you taught me about love in the village, I'm gonna show you how we do it downtown." And I got him up in me— he's going, "Oh, God, no, oh, God forgive her." Maybe if he'd said, Oh, God, forgive *me*—and I told him, "And I'm gonna write you a little story, Tom—that I want you to treasure, 'cause I get about three thousand dollars for something like this." And I took that nice indelible pen and took his shirt and wiped the sweat off his pretty blank white hairless chest and wrote: "Once there was a little girl whose guardian came to see her in the night." Keeping my hips going and writing was like trying to rub your stomach and pat your head. He's bucking around, yelling, "You're not really writin' that, don't mark me up." I said, "Oh, honey, you marked me up." My story went something like—I'm saying it aloud, writing: "He liked to put his hands on her adolescent breasts to excite himself and he liked to rub his hot dick on her red cheeks—her cheeks must have felt like flames. And when he got so hot and hard he couldn't stand it any longer he'd put it in her mouth to cool himself off and pump till he came. And that's how he took care of his little ward. And that's how his little ward took care of him." *(Beat.)* Probably a little more Dickensian than most of my work. Of course he was screaming and bucking. I wasn't proud of my penmanship, but under the circumstances—and I went slow enough to make sure it was legible. Then he was trying not to come. Saying, "Stop it, don't do that. I don't do that anymore. I was drunk. It was the devil, darlin'," wailing like a revivalist and I said, "When you come Daddy, let's both yell 'Oh, yes,'" but I yelled, "Oh, yes," and he yelled, "Oh, God!" I lay down stretched out, against his chest. I told him, "All those other times were for you, Daddy, but this one was for me." *(Beat.)* So I got my overnight bag and got the car keys that had fallen out of his pocket onto the rug. And left him there, hog-tied and inscribed in the middle of the floor. Naked as the day he was born—looking like the pot-gutted tattooed man. I said, "Thank you, Tom." Then I stood in the doorway for a long while like he used to do. Only he wasn't pretending to be asleep, he was twisting around on the rug, yelling, "Untie me, damnit. Diane, where do you think you're agoin'? Don't leave me here all marked up." I went out to the car, drove it to the airport, and left it there.

NASTY RUMORS AND FINAL REMARKS by Susan Miller

MAX, a woman in her forties, talks to her female lover, Raleigh, who is in a coma.

SCENE: A hospital room.

TIME: The present.

MAX: The nurse said I could have a couple of words with you. I'll bet you just love that. Someone else giving me permission to come and go. Breaks every rule in the house, doesn't it? Listen, I can't find your Tiffany earrings anywhere. If I do, should I give them to Cat? Not that I've been very successful at finding Cat. But don't worry, she usually leaves some kind of trail. We're having a bitch of a time here with all your worldly goods, such as they are. I'm probably going to sell my car and buy yours from the kids. They could use the money. And besides, I like the way your car smells. As far as the taxes and bills and all that business shit, Nicky's got a good lawyer...except you did stuff the Sears bill between pages 104 and 105 of Tennessee Williams' *Collected Plays*, so God knows where the Dept. of Water and Power will show up. Now all of this is just in case. This does not mean you have to take it seriously. You can change your mind. I'll keep my crummy car. I'm only telling you these things so you won't be worried about details. But you can sit right up and shock the hell out of everyone, as far as I'm concerned. This place could use a little slap in the face, you know. Or...I mean, if that's too hard, right now, just move your index finger. Curse. Whatever. All miracles accepted. Shit, I believe in miracles. Clap you hands if you believe...
(Pause)
This is terrific. I could sit here all day and talk, repeat all my old stories and you can't even tell me to shut up. Except you aren't laughing and that's really what kept me talking all these years.
(Pause)
Actually, I'd love to hear you say SHUT UP. Go on, go ahead. Just for old times sake. Give it to me good. C'mon. SHUT UP, MAX.

Huh? How about it...please. Please tell me to shut the fuck up!

(Pause)

God, you're beautiful. You're not supposed to be that beautiful. This is intensive care, remember?

NIGHT SKY by Susan Yankowitz

A female astronomy teacher struggles to regain her speech after getting hit by a car and becoming aphasic, and, literally, loses the ability to speak.

Here we witness Anna, before her accident, as she stands within a star-filled night sky, completing a lecture to her class.

SCENE: A podium.

TIME: The present.

ANNA: ...But do you realize that what we see represents only ten percent—possibly only one percent—of what exists? Most of the universe is hidden, invisible to us still, a mysterious absence. We know very little. Even the most basic insights elude us. How many stars are there, and how do we know there aren't more? Why do the planets spin, and if they didn't spin, where would they go? Are we one of many universes, or is there only this one universe? If a black hole is truly black, and if it really is a hole, how can we be sure it's there? And within all that dark matter, somewhere, does life exist? *(Pause.)* Please consider these questions for your next class. Oh, that reminds me: the word "consider" means literally "with the stars." Study the language. You probably don't know that people in the seventeenth century died in droves from a disease called "planet." Or that when you miss a class because you have the flu—influenza—your illness derives from the Italian for "astral influence." And if your friend calls you a "schlemazel" for spilling ink on your exam, are you aware that's Yiddish for someone born under an unlucky star? Then there's a word your generation uses every day—"disaster!" and what does it actually mean? Bad star! *(Steps down from the podium.)* Dismissed!

NON-BRIDALED PASSION (from *A...My Name Is Still Alice*) by
Kate Shein

**A WOMAN, in her thirties, walks up to a Bridal Registry Consultant,
standing behind a counter.**

**SCENE: The Bridal Registry at one of the finer department stores. In the
background we hear cash registers pinging and low volume Muzak.**

TIME: The present.

WOMAN: Excuse me; are you the registry consultant? Well, I'm
here to register! For gifts. This is a really big step for me; I'm very
excited! I'll bet you hear that a lot, don't you? ...When is the happy
event?... Oh, you mean *wedding date*. There isn't one. I'm not getting
married. I'll probably never get married. But, I need things, and I think
registering is a good way for me to learn to receive. ...Yes, I know this
is the *Bridal* Registry, and that you only register *brides*. Frankly, I find
that a bit discriminatory. I'm here to register and I really don't want
any hassle. ...No, no, don't get the manager...I am *not* trying to cause
trouble. LOOK, for months now I've been buying gifts for all of my
friends who've been getting married. It's an epidemic. There's been a
slew of weddings, not to mention showers, lately, and I've attended all
of them, brought gifts to every event.

It's not that I begrudge them their happiness, not at all—I'm a
very supportive person. It's just that lately I've been feeling that
something's a little out of whack, you know, sort of off-balance; and
yesterday, while I was attaching tiny silver bells to a spice rack for my
friends, Howie and Wendy, this voice inside my head started
screaming at me. It said, "Schmuck! Why do you keep buying presents
for people who have already found everything they want?" Or words
to that effect. I don't remember exactly. I do recall that the voice
sounded resentful. And I had to agree with it. I mean, isn't it enough
that they were lucky and found each other? That they fell in love and
made a commitment? That they'll be splitting the rent and filing
jointly? My God, they've found someone who'll give them a FOOT
MASSAGE whenever they want! They've already won the

sweepstakes, why do they get the doorprizes too? Why do they get to register for things like...like...like a cookie jar shaped like a giant eggplant, or a set of "really good knives"? THEY'RE BECOMING A TWO-INCOME FAMILY FOR CHRISTSAKE, WHY CAN'T THEY BUY THEIR OWN KNIVES???!!! Now then. I need things. I am not getting married and I need things. I need better towels. Matching luggage. A pasta machine. And sterling silver candlesticks—since I was five years old, my grandmother promised me hers the day I got married. Well, I didn't get married, and last month they went to my cousin Marcy, who did. Why? Why do you only get family heirlooms if you wed? It's no damn fair. Candlesticks! Put me down for two pairs! Come on, just do it! You registered Ann and Deena, Becky, Jane and Cindy, I *insist* on registering too! I *know* I'm single. I confront that fact every day of my life. It's fine! I LIKE it! But I'm not staying single without the same material goods as my married friends. *My ship is coming in if I have to tow it myself*! Do you really want to know when the happy event is? It's a week from Saturday. That's the day I'm throwing a shower for myself, officially announcing a life of singlehood. And the beauty of it is, I won't have to return anything if it doesn't work out!

OLEANNA by David Mamet

You can call it a riff on the Anita Hill-Clarence Thomas controversy or a particularly virulent battle in the war between women and men. *Oleanna* is deceptively simple in plot and only becomes complicated when you try to figure out exactly what happened. A lot is said, but a lot more is insinuated and even more is to be discussed and argued about.

CAROL, a student of twenty, has come to John, a forty-year-old teacher, because she is failing his course. John tries to soothe Carol and find out how to help her. He is by turns concerned and anxious to get rid of her. Later, John discovers that Carol has reported him to the tenure committee as an elitist, sexist, purveyor of pornographic stories, and a physical harasser to boot. Eventually, she raises the charge of attempted rape. When John denies the charge, Carol responds.

SCENE: John's office.

TIME: The present.

CAROL: How can you *deny* it. You did it to me. *Here.* You *did…* You *confess.* You love the Power. To *deviate.* To *invent,* to transgress…to *transgress* whatever norms have been established for us. And you think it's charming to "question" in yourself this taste to mock and destroy. But you should question it. Professor. And you pick those things which you feel *advance* you: publication, *tenure,* and the steps to get them you call "harmless rituals." And you perform those steps. Although you say it is hypocrisy. But to the aspirations of your students. Of *hardworking students,* who come here, who *slave* to come here—you have no idea what it cost me to come to this school—you *mock* us. You call education "hazing," and from your so-protected, so-elitist seat you hold our confusion as a *joke,* and our hopes and efforts with it. Then you sit there and say "what have I done?" And ask me to understand that you have aspirations too. But I tell you. I tell you. That you are vile. And that you are exploitative. And if you possess one ounce of that inner honesty you describe in your book, you can look in yourself and see those things that I see. And you can find revulsion equal to my own. Good day. *(She prepares to leave then room.)*

ONE NAKED WOMAN AND A FULLY CLOTHED MAN by Diana Amsterdam

JANET, thirties, watches a movie with her husband Robert and we hear her thoughts.

SCENE: A movie theatre.

TIME: The present.

JANET: I am that woman on the screen. I am going to go away soon. And have numerous big adventures. I'm going to stay in a hotel just like that one, and wear a silk blouse just like that one. I'm still young. I'm still attractive. Look how he looks at her. Nobody knows how to look at a woman better than my Robert knows how to look at a woman.

(JANET turns to look at ROBERT, and stares at him so hard that he looks at her, smiles, pats her hand, turns back to the screen. She turns back to the screen.)

JANET: Omigod! When did that happen? Why do they do this to people? There's probably one woman in this entire theatre who looks like that and that one woman is sitting up tall and proud while the rest of us are shrinking. You gotta admit they're beautiful, though. Beautiful breasts are beautiful. The female form is beautiful. I have a female form. Robert. Don't look. It's just that my female form has had three children, my breasts have nursed three fat babies, my breasts have served as pacifiers and teething rings—My breasts are real breasts—Real. Saggy. Ruined. Don't look! He's looking. I wonder if he's noticing. Comparing her breasts to mine— *(She grabs a handful of popcorn, stuffs it in her mouth, several kernels fall onto her bosom. She gives a little shriek.)*

[THE MOVIEGOERS: Shhh!]

(JANET rummages in her dress for the various kernels of popcorn. ROBERT glances at her.)

JANET: *(In actual dialogue, to ROBERT. Whispers as she rummages in her dress.)* Darling, remind me to find Jason's galoshes when we get home.

(JANET and ROBERT turn back to the movie.)

JANET: How much footage can you take of one woman's breasts? So when she throws up her arms they bobble up and down, big deal, toss up a cabbage that comes down, too, why don't they show us five minutes of cole slaw? Slow motion. Only a male director would do this. Only a male director would ever assume that an entire audience would be interested in fifteen minutes of footage of one woman's breasts. *(She glances around the theatre.)* And he's right. The entire audience is glued to that screen. Every last eye in the place, glued. When he was showing footage of the majestic Alps, everyone was fidgeting but plaster a coupla boobies up there and people stop breathing. I can understand it with the men. But you'd think the women would rebel. You'd think the women would turn and talk to one another, show snapshots of our children, or get up on the seats and dance, *something.* I'd like to see 500 men sit like house plants for 25 minutes while some female director exhibits the bobbling capacity of the male penis in slow motion. Sure. I'm afraid to look at him. His lips are probably parted. There's probably a thin stream of drool oozing from his mouth.

(JANET reaches over to touch ROBERT's lips. He kisses her fingertips.)

JANET: I'm such a fool. He's not thinking about that woman's breasts at all, he's thinking about me, he's thinking about how beautiful it is to be sitting next to a woman whose breasts have been used for the furtherance of life, who has really made something of her breasts.

[*(ROBERT kisses the empty air.)*]

JANET: Reflex.

(JANET and ROBERT sit and watch the movie. ROBERT has stopped eating popcorn.)

JANET: Popcorn, dear?

PARTY TIME by Harold Pinter

A group of wealthy socialites are drinking and talkings about a new healthclub. MELISSA is seventy.

SCENE: A large room. Sofas, armchair, etc. People sitting, standing. A waiter with a drink tray. Spasmodic party music throughout the play.

TIME: The present.

MELISSA: Can I subscribe to all that has just been said?

(Pause.)

I would like to subscribe to all that has just been said. I would like to add my voice. I have belonged to many tennis and swimming clubs. Many tennis and swimming clubs. And at some of these clubs I first met some of my dearest friends. All of them are now dead. Every friend I ever had. Or ever met. Is dead. They are all of them dead. Every single one of them. I have absolutely not one left. None are left. Nothing is left. What was it all for? The tennis and the swimming clubs? What was it all for? What?

(Silence.)

But the clubs died too and rightly so. I mean there is a distinction to be made. My friends went the way of all flesh and I don't regret their passing. They weren't my friends anyway. I couldn't stand half of them. But the clubs! The clubs died, the swimming and the tennis clubs died because they were based on ideas which had no moral foundation, no moral foundation whatsoever. But *our* club, *our* club— is a club which is activated, which is inspired by a moral sense, a moral awareness, a set of moral values which is—I have to say— unshakeable, rigorous, fundamental, constant. Thank you.

POWER FAILURE by Larry Gelbart

In this brilliant black comedy, every single character is revealed to be a hypocrite. COYNE, a female journalist in her thirties, is writing a book on Will, a convicted murderer who maintains his innocence. Earlier, we have seen her with Will on death row, sympathetically chronicling his version of events.

Coyne is at home with her proctologist husband as they dress for a party. Her husband innocently asks her "When did you make your film deal?" Coyne goes ballistic.

SCENE: An elegant bedroom.

TIME: The present.

COYNE: Sweetheart, don't ever say that again. You are never to repeat that phrase outside this room. Ever. To anyone. You are not to put the words "picture" and "deal" together in the same sentence, not even in the same paragraph, until after his execution. Verity made me swear I'd tell no one. The way she's set it up, Warner's is not going to sign my contract with them until after the word "dead" on Will's certificate, they write in "as a doornail." If he finds out about it now, if he even smells a hint of it, his agent is going to want all kinds of approvals for him. Credit. Some kind of profit participation. Who knows what kind of involvement? The truth is, once he butchered his family, his work was finished. Now, he's got to let go; let the rest of us get on with things. Being guilty of killing your wife and daughters doesn't automatically make someone an executive producer, you know, or a whole lot more people would be doing it.

RED SCARE ON SUNSET by Charles Busch

PAT PILFORD, an attractive blonde radio columnist in her thirties and former virulent anti-communist has suddenly become a stooge for the party. She is visiting film star Mary Dale, who has overdosed on sleeping pills. Pat makes a startling confession when Mary pumps her for information.

SCENE: A hospital in Hollywood, California.

TIME: 1951.

PAT: *(Breaks down.)* NO, no, no, no, no. I hate the communists. I'd like to see them all exterminated. It's Mitchell Drake...He's blackmailing me. [FRANK: What's he got on you?] Years ago in New York, I was very much in love with the son of a bitch. Love. Whoever thought love could be a dirty word. I was obsessed with him. I was no longer a woman of achievement, but a thing. I abandoned all sense of decency. I was in his thrall. Always that penis staring at me, taunting me! Mocking me! One night he got me drunk and took photos of me performing some of the most repugnant acts a woman could do. [MARY: *(With genuine interest.)* For instance?] To even tell you would be to insult you. Now he intends to distribute them nationally unless I remain a commie tool.

RED SCARE ON SUNSET by Charles Busch

MARTA TOWERS, a pretty young film actress in her thirties, demure but with an inner fire, is forced to reveal, under the questioning of R.G. Nelson, a "director," her true identity.

SCENE: The Yetta Felson Acting Studios, specializing in teaching the Method but in reality a communist cell.

TIME: 1951.

MARTA: *(Violently.)* Yes! I am Commissar Olga Shumsky! And yes, I killed Marta Towers, the simpering little fool. I shared a quesadilla with her at a truck stop, and endured her recitation of Juliet's potion scene in her revolting Oklahoma twang. It was simple slipping the arsenic that turned her tequila sunrise into a sunset. I became the respected actress she'd never be. The New York critics rhapsodized over my solo "Three Sisters." I should have become a major film star but the studios were too busy giving the build up to clap-ridden whores with dubbed voices!

(Ominous MUSIC begins.)

You think you've stopped us, you haven't scratched the surface. We're everywhere, getting stronger, getting three-picture deals and producer credit. Listen, hear the drums beating, pounding as we march down Hollywood Boulevard, trampling over the faded names of the soon to be forgotten stars. March! March! Stamp on the infidels, the agents, the bloodsuckers, the columnists! March! March! [R.G.: *(To Yetta.)* Send her to the psychopathic ward. *(YETTA begins to lead MARTA away.)*] *(Clearly insane.)* Who am I? I'm a Soviet agent...No, I'm an actress. I'm a Soviet agent...No, I'm a seagull. Squawk! Squawk! Masha, want a cracker?

RED SCARE ON SUNSET by Charles Busch

MARY DALE, an ageless Scarlett O'Hara-like film star, in a lovely white dress and straw boater, addresses the U.S. Senate. She has come to inform on the communist activities of just about everybody she knows, including Frank Taggart, her husband.

SCENE: The U.S. Senate.

TIME: 1951.

MARY: *(Standing at podium with microphones UC.)* Senators, gentlemen, I stand before this august body terribly humbled. Only in America could a young girl raised by struggling farmers in Indiana grow up to be a movie star and also able to speak to a distinguished panel of Senators and may I add, most handsome. The world is so complicated today. A girl doesn't know which way to turn. One wants to do the correct thing. But what is the correct thing? What's smart today, could be dumb tomorrow. But I had a dream about Lady Godiva, which is my latest film and I cordially invite all of you to the premiere at the Pantages. And from that dream I learned to apply the simple answers of a bygone era to the complicated questions of today. And that is why I am here before this congressional investigation to provide you with a list of names to aid you in your noble hunt to route out the red menace. Together with God's help we can make sure that these people never work again. *(She opens envelope.)* My this is very exciting. *(She takes list out of envelope.)* I name Marlo Towers, Bertram Barker...*(She pauses for a moment, hesitantly.)* and because I love him, Frank Taggart. *(Regaining her sense of purpose.)* From the student roster of the Yetta Felson Studio, I name Betty Foster, Jeff Patterson, Morris Kleiner, Mildred Pishkin, Lona Myers, Anthony Reaci, Rudy Abbotelli, Howard Mandlebaum, June Sycoff...

SCRUPLES by Jon Jory

Four actresses wait for their final call-back auditions.

MRS. DOBBS, an efficient woman in a suit, enters.

SCENE: A corporate reception area.

TIME: The present.

MRS. DOBBS: *(Pleasant, straight-forward, and without artifice.)* Good morning. [LOIS: Good morning. JANE: Good morning. *(They all look at MARTI. She waves.)*] I am glad to see you, Lois, Jane, and Marti. I am Letitia Dobbs. [JANE: Hello, Mrs. Dobbs. LOIS: Hello, Letitia. MARTI: *(A pause.)* Hi.] I handle East Coast casting for Nightsilk pantyhose. The three of you, selected from hundreds of young women, are our final callbacks not for simply a commercial but for a series of commercials filmed over a two-year period, which the winner will find very, very, very, very, very, very lucrative. Nightsilk, realizing that its products could be categorized as trivial and cognizant that unpopular animal research is crucial to developing world-class pantyhose is donating two cents a pair to African famine relief, which on our annual sales of over a billion dollars will provide over two million dollars of food supplies, so you will be not only body parts but spokespersons and benefactors. Thus, while only your legs will be filmed, we will be wanting you to do a good deal of speaking and traveling on our behalf. Please remember also that legs are not simply sculptural, not simply matter. There are millions of technically attractive legs, but they can be more, much more. Legs can be infused with a sense of self and spirit which animates them on camera and communicates to the viewer with damaged self-esteem new goals and new hope. A beautiful soul makes beautiful legs, and Nightsilk, by enhancing the leg, enhances the soul. [(*JANE applauds.*)] Thank you. We are, mincing no words, looking for an uncommon woman for an uncommon job in uncommon times. The callback will begin with a forty-minute in-depth interview exploring your world view and your attitudes toward both our project and our product. Then, of course, in a monitored environment we will be asking you to take off your clothes. Please relax and center yourself for this exciting and challenging process. My assistant, Mr. Skiles will be around shortly with fruit frappes and nibbles. Nightsilk pantyhose apologizes that we are running...(*Checks her watch.*) forty minutes behind schedule, we know your time is valuable. I can tell by speaking with you that you are lovely and intelligent young women with caring and remarkable parents. Are there any questions?

SEARCH AND DESTROY by Howard Korder

Martin Mirkheim, a would-be movie producer, wants to option a novel by an L. Ron Hubbard-type guru. He flies in to propose a deal but he can't get in to see the writer, so he plays up to the man's receptionist, MARIE, a seemingly mousie type in her early twenties. It turns out that she's written a movie script. At dinner later, she pitches him her script.

SCENE: An airport snack bar.

TIME: The present.

MARIE: Everybody's dead all over. Okay. She's caught. The spinesucker has her pinned against the wall. With his other hand he cracks open her boyfriend's head and smears his brains all over her tits. Okay. The elevator's stuck between floors. This thing comes out of him like a gangrene penis with a lobster claw and starts burrowing into her. The pain's unbearable. Okay. Finally she manages to reach the switch on the radial saw and rips it into him. But he just smiles, okay, his stomach opens up and he absorbs it, like he does and goes on pumping her up. She's gonna die, that's all. *Except* inside him the saw's still going, spinning around, he starts shaking and there's a, what do you, close shot, yeah, and the saw rips out of his chest, there's this explosion of meat and pus pouring out like from a fire hose, he climbs on her and tries to shove the penis claw down her throat, okay, but she hacks it off with the saw okay he goes shooting back against the glass door okay they break he falls five floors, onto the metal spike in the fountain it goes straight through his face, his brains spurt out and slide into the water like fresh cum okay. He's dead, he's dead, he's finally fucking dead. She walks away that's the end.

SENSIBILITY AND SENSE by Richard Nelson

This play contrasts the lives of American intellectuals of the left today with their idealistic counterparts in the 1930's.

THERESE, in her twenties, tells her houseguests about her husband.

SCENE: The living room of a large wooden vacation home in the Adirondack Mountains. Accessible only by boat, the house and its various cabins overlook a large lake.

TIME: 1937.

THERESE: Harvey and I have been having sort of a hard time of it lately. [EDWARD: I'm sorry.] Don't be. *(Short pause.)* [ELINOR: He's not up—?] Here? No. *(Beat.)* Not this week. [ELINOR: Oh.] It's all my fault really. I never should have introduced him to my friend, Josie. See—she was my friend first. I met her first. *(Beat.)* Beautiful girl. We'd spent the whole summer camping together in Montana. The sky out there. It's everything they say it is. It's so romantic. *(Beat.)* You and your friend, Marianne, should try camping out there sometime. [ELINOR: Yeh.] Josie and I had met in a bar in Chicago. I was changing trains. I mean, who knew that this girl with those big brown eyes could also type? *(Smiles to herself.)* I don't know how it happened, but somehow Harvey made her his secretary. She travels with him all the time now. Sometimes I go along too—but I find that sort of thing really confusing. Anyway, instead of trying to argue me out of it, Harvey got me a press card from *Time Life*. He said that was something he could do for me. So off I went to Spain. *(Short pause.)* I guess what it comes down to is he called my bluff. *(Short pause.)* On the other hand I've often wondered if Harvey didn't see it as a plus— my being over there fighting the fascists. When you're dealing with defense contracts all the time like he is, having some tie to someone with a belief, well, it helps create the illusion that there is more to you than just greed. I don't know. *(Drinks down her drink.)* One more and then let's open the wine. *(EDWARD takes her glass. MARIANNE is at the porch door looking in. She holds a lantern.)* What are you three, still in college or what? [MARIANNE: No. *(EDWARD and ELINOR turn to her, seeing her there for the first time.)* No, we're not in—] *(Not listening)* Speaking of wine. Do you know how they open wine bottles in Spain? Not all bottles. I only saw this once, but— *(Beat.)* They take a dog. I saw them do this with a collie. Part collie. And they take the dog's penis and tape it to the top of the bottle and then they start rubbing its balls and the idea, see, is that the erection will push in the cork. *(Laughs to herself.)* Never saw it work. *(Beat.)* There are things happening in Spain that you or I never even imagined. *(EDWARD hands her her drink.)* Thank you. We should be ready in just a few minutes. *(Throughout the rest of the scene THERESE goes back and forth from the kitchen bringing out dishes, glasses, etc.)* There was a particular *cabo*—that's corporal. She was the one who convinced me to join the woman's militia. A huge woman. She was Russian. *(Beat.)* Burgundy OK with everyone? *(Beat.)* And she had us—the women—out chopping wood in the forest one morning. Except for these two English comrades who were going to stand guard between us and the line, we all had set down our rifles so we could chop. We needed the wood. *(Beat.)* It gets pretty damn cold in Spain in January. And now it is bitter cold. *(Beat.)* Suddenly we see this man come through the woods. We all stop and freeze. The two with their guns—the English girls from Manchester—point them. Then, this man, unaware that here are forty or so young women with axes a few yards away from him, he pulls down his pants and squats. *(Beat.)* Well, the Russian comrade—the *cabo*—she gestures for none of us to move, and she silently picks up her gun, and then—she screams: "Stand up!" *(Beat.)* In Spanish. *(Beat.)* The man stands up, with his pants now—And you see his face as he sees himself standing there, and we are a crowd of women not only with rifles but also with these very sharp axes. *(Laughs to herself as she continues to serve the meal.)* I think he was an anarchist actually. POUM most likely. You should have seen his boots—nothing really left of them. Also he had a lot of body hair—so he looked like a farmer, not a fascist. So— POUM. Anyway, the *cabo,* she goes up to him and without so much as hesitating—*(Smiles to herself.)* She grabs ahold of his penis and gives it a huge tug. *(Pours the soup.)* And he's on the ground now and she says—"I wanted to ring your bell." *(Laughs to herself.)* In Spanish she says this. "Ring your bell." *(Beat.)* That's an expression we had, there was a song—it's a pun really. *(Beat.)* It was very funny. *(Beat.)* That's war for you. *(Beat.)* That and body lice. *(Beat.)* For some reason international proletarian solidarity and body lice will be forever linked in my mind. *(Beat.)* Dinner is served. Eddie, do you want to open the wine?

SEPARATION by Tom Kempinski

An aspiring actress in New York who has a degenerative bone disease and uses crutches strikes up a bizarre long-distance relationship with a playwright in London, who is afraid to leave his apartment. Their telephone conversations blossom into a hesitant and troubled romance, spanning two cities and two frightened people's hearts.

SARAH, twenty to thirty, on the phone, tells Joe that she has been cast in a new play. He accuses her of betraying him by taking a role written by someone else. Earlier, he prevented her from acquiring rights to produce his play in San Francisco. Now her bitter resentment at his attack comes pouring out.

SCENE: Sarah's New York City apartment.

TIME: The present.

SARAH: You bastard!, you absolute bastard!...*(JOE is rigid, open-mouthed.)* I'm in PAIN again, and it could be a relapse and I don't know if it is and the doctor doesn't know and I didn't want to load it onto you, so I didn't tell you and *THAT'S* why I haven't been to see you yet, you *bastard,* and I didn't come to you and say I'd make you happy, I didn't come and say I'd give you peace, love, and paradise, I phoned you up for the play, I came for the God-damn play and I said so. I was straight with you, I've always been straight with you, you bastard, and then we *did* become friends, we *did,* and you became...you became...*(She is on the point of crying, but won't show him, because she wants to stay angry, so she shouts loudly.)* MY DOOR-BELL'S RINGING, YOU STAY THERE YOU HEAR ME, YOU STAY THERE!! *(As JOE stands rigid with shock and shame she puts her hand over the mouthpiece and holds it to herself, bending forward slightly with the phone clasped to her middle. She tightens her mouth to hold back the tears, though a few get through...)* Bastard...Bastards...*(She sits on the bed and when she feels she has the sorrow-part sufficiently under control she continues, just as angry but a little more control putting the phone back to her mouth.)* Yes, we heard a lot about your problems, Joe, and I know you're struggling, I know you're trying to get out from under, but it takes two to tango, my friend, so let me *tell* you about my male friends you're always making snidey enquiries about, because from thirteen when I had my first attack I have needed strong men, Joe, strong doctors to save my life and a strong father to wheel me around, and I was just a body, I was just the victim and they did all the living for me. And then when the attack passed in my teens I was still afraid to stand up for myself in case the promised relapse came and I needed the strong men again, so I never stood up to my father, I never tangled with him so I was no use to him at all, I was his girl, but I wasn't the girl he wanted...*(She's gone quiet.)* And then I became a woman, and I went out with strong men and kept my mouth shut. And then seven years ago I *did* have the big relapse and after I got better, that is after I got out of the hospital a semi-basket case, the strong and capable men stood in line to look after me...*(Shouts)* but they weren't strong men! They weren't, they were the screw-the-rubber-doll brigade, they wanted to help me upstairs and into cars and run my life but *(She rises)* God help me if I suggested which restaurant to go to or any other sign of independence because they *wanted* me weak, that's what they *liked* about me, they *liked* my *miserable illness*...*(Quiet)* and then I met you, Joe, *(Shouts)* and you needed me, you need me, you big, dumb bastard, you need me desperately, you stupid asshole!...*(She stops, breathless, but goes on soon, driven by her need for him. Quieter)* Yes. You needed me. And suddenly I was a somebody after all. Some poor, screwed-up, intelligent, funny writer needed me...*(Shouts)* because I kept you going on the end of this God-damn 'phone, I kept you out of desperation and that is a *valuable deed*...*(Quiet, matter-of-fact)* and what do you do, you deliberately screw-up San Francisco for me in some childish attempt to stop me getting away, *(half-laugh)* when I didn't want to get away at all. I was coming after you...*(She pauses. Weakly starts an excuse.)* [JOE: I don't think I...] *(Interrupts, shouts)* You shut up, you shut up, you liar, you listen!...*(Deliberate)* You screwed up San Francisco for me to try and keep me, and now I've got this new play you say, "I give you a choice, Sarah Wise, stay in the rubber-doll-paralyzed necrophilia league and I accept you, or be the struggling-to-be-a-human-being type and I throw you out..." *(Shouts)* Well you will stop this! You will stop this immediately now, you need me and you will let me help you and mean something and help you write and have my place, you absolute, total, complete utter bastard!!...

SERVY-N-BERNICE 4EVER BY Seth Zvi Rosenfeld

BERNICE, a black woman in her early twenties, has escaped the life of Alphabet City in New York by going to college in Boston. She has also left her old boyfriend Servy when he was sent to prison. Now that he's out she invites him to come over. Servy quickly discovers that she has lied a) to her new friends about her family, saying they're professional

people, and b) to her mother about school.

SCENE: A studio apartment in Backbay Boston.

TIME: The present.

(BERNICE takes picture of her father and stares at it)
BERNICE: He was so proud that I had a scholarship to go to college that on my eighteenth birthday, one week before I left to go to college my father took me to Tiffany's. He wanted me to have something to remember him by. I said, "Daddy I know you don't have money to buy something expensive." He told me to pick out anything I wanted. I picked out the least expensive ring I could find. It was a thin gold ring with tiny chips of diamonds and rubies. I showed it to my father, he loved it, we walked right up to the counter just as proud as could be because he was my daddy and I was his baby and we were having this moment, right. Now the salesman at the counter was nervous because my father looked like a dope fiend and he knew damn well that he wasn't supposed to be in no Tiffany's buyin' no ring for his daughter's birthday. He says, "is this cash or charge," my father gave him this credit card. The salesman took the card and was gone a long time, my father was sweating, the man came back with the security guard and they took my father away...Next time I saw him I was wearing black and he was the man in the pine box.
...I wonder what that nigga would say if he knew I failed out of college and lost that scholarship.

SMOKE ON THE MOUNTAIN by Connie Ray, conceived by Alan Bailey

A Saturday Night Gospel Sing featuring the Sanders Family in their first appearance on the gospel circuit in five years.

DENISE SANDERS, twenty-three, addresses the congregation.

SCENE: The Mount Pleasant Baptist Church in the depressed factory town of Mount Pleasant, North Carolina.

TIME: 1938.

DENISE: Have you ever been to a movie-house? I have—six times—with my Mama and Daddy's permission. *(VERA and BURL decide to let her speak and move upstage.)* And it has changed my life. Sitting in the dark watching the picture stars fall in love and get in trouble while wearing evening gowns. Did y'all see *Three Comrades?* When Margaret Sullivan died that terrible death in that long, shiny gown, I had to go to bed for two days.

I read about it in the Asheville *Citizen*. This man, this Mr. Selznick, says he's looking for a new girl. "The best girl that shows up will play the part willy-nilly." And I just know he's talking about me. They're searching high and low for Scarlett, and I'm sitting right outside Siler City. This is my year off from Bible School. I got plenty of time to make a picture. The paper says he'll be in Charlotte on Friday the 14th. Valentime's Day! They're looking for an unknown: young and charged with electricity.

I sneak a tablecloth and fashion myself a Hollywood dress—snow white with a red felt heart here *(Over her heart.)* for the Day.

I slip off and buy the bus ticket. I sit in the chicken house and practice "Fiddle-dee-dee." When Valentime's came, I was up at the crack. My sister June had just bought a new pocketbook that matched my Hollywood shoes, and I snatched it up as I stole out of the house.

[*(At the mention of her name, JUNE goes rigid with fear of being linked to the deed. If she could crawl under the floorboards she would.)*]

And when I got to the bus stop, I saw before me...there standing before me...every girl in my community.

The bus pulled up, and we filed on. There were ten or fifteen girls on from Bushy Mountain already. Every stop, more girls pile on. We pull into Charlotte not speaking a word. They march us in ten to a row. Mr. Selznick is sitting behind a desk with his hand held up to his face like this. *(Demonstrates.)* Two little men sit by his side and whisper things in his ear like the Last Supper picture.

[BURL: Denise...honey.]

(PASTOR OGLETHORPE is scandalized. His love is short-lived.)

Mr. Selznick looks up and down the line, and he says, "You, little girl with the heart, you stay."

I go, and I stand before him, and he asks me my name, and where

I'm from, and how old I am, and have I ever been to Charlotte before, and was I planning on staying overnight. Friendly things like that. He says I am delightful. That if he didn't know better, he'd swear I was a Rockette. I didn't even know what a Rockette *was* back then. He says, "I'll be in touch." And when I looked up from writing down my address—he winked at me.

On the bus home, everybody's crying. But me. "I'll be in touch!" He's gonna write me! I could be the new girl! I'd be perfect as Scarlett! I find a pack of violet candy in June's purse, and I eat the whole thing in celebration.

[JUNE: *(Jumps up.)* I'd like to say that I didn't know anything about this. *(Sits.)*]

But you see, yesterday marked four months. And Mr. Selznick hasn't been in touch. I'm pretty sure I'm not gonna be Scarlett. The paper says they gave the part to Paulette Goddard. She'll be good. *(Starts to cry.)* I know this has to do with Jesus and my soul in some way. My mama and daddy wanted me to say something and...I know I lapsed. My sins are many and easy to count.

I'm powerfully sorry for not honoring my Mother and Father. For snatching my sister's hard-gotten belonging and eating what was in it. But as far as the sin to myself, I truly haven't figured that out yet. I pray I will, and I know Jesus hears my prayers.

[*(BURL and PASTOR OGLETHORPE stand.)* BURL: Thank you, honey. *(When DENISE begins speaking again, BURL and PASTOR OGLETHORPE quickly sit.)*]

I'm a nice girl from a nice family that wraps me in a sheet of love every day.

(BURL and PASTOR OGLETHORPE stand again. DENISE starts to move back upstage. She has another thought and comes back. BURL and PASTOR OGLETHORPE sit again.)

I am thankful for all the gifts God has given me. But I believe a Christian shouldn't have to see Walt Disney movies only. Though I did see *Snow White and the Seven Dwarfs*, and it was so good, I'll never get over it.

A SOUVENIR OF POMPEII by Sari Bodi

HELEN, twenties or thirties. has just kidnapped a newborn baby from the hospital and proudly brings it home to her husband, Sam. Sam is horrified and calls the police. When the police arrive, Sam has locked himself in the bedroom to protect the baby, while Helen sits in a rocking chair grasping a Pompeian statuette to her breast.

SCENE: Helen's living room.

TIME: The present.

HELEN: This souvenir disrupted my life. It's just a small statuette from the ruins of Pompeii that I bought when Sam and I vacationed there. In Pompeii, you can see people encased for eternity in the ashes of an erupting Mount Vesuvius, trapped in 79 A.D. in whatever they were doing in the last seconds of their lives. My statuette is of a woman crouched in the position of what looks like giving birth. And the more I looked at this statuette, the more I realized it was me, trapped forever in the position of waiting to give birth. Sam avoided this statue. He didn't want to think about its significance. So night after night, year after year, Sam and I groped for each other across wrinkled sheets and pale flesh, hoping to create life. And always between us was the blame, that one of us was causing the future to halt, trapping us forever in the present.

So yesterday, I went to see Dr. Charness. Mothers had recommended him. Mothers of healthy babies who would knock on my door to supply endless names of fertility specialists as well as allow me to touch their babies. Because my neighbors believed that touching babies would create new ones. So yesterday, I held ten babies and then went to Dr. Charness, a man who had created infant cells in the bodies of countless neighborhood women across Westchester. And as Dr. Charness began the usual poking and prodding inside my body, I began to think of myself as an archeological dig like the one they began in 1748 when they discovered that first pottery shard in Pompeii. But it was when Dr. Charness finally stopped his excavating, and turned to me and said, "You will never be able to bear children." It was when that happened...when he was explaining to me in the black and whiteness of medical rules, that I discovered that I preferred the world in more colorful ways. I focused on the woman's anatomy chart on his wall, on the bright pink and blue ovaries, uterus and fallopian tubes whose cheerful shapes reminded me of a Georgia O'Keefe painting. And so by bringing those colors into my mind, I didn't hear the black and whiteness of Dr. Charness' words. Instead what I heard was, "Ah hah! We've discovered what is wrong. This is very curious, but it seems that you do not possess human eggs. Your eggs are of the pink-billed, blue throated woodpecker. I'm afraid that you'll just have to find one of these in the male variety to mate with." So armed with this knowledge, I made my way to the nearest tree, and began knocking my nose against the bark. And sure enough, he flew down. And I tell you, if you haven't tried sex with a woodpecker, it is fabulous. All that vibration. And last night as Sam and I were continuing our passionless embracing, I saw myself dancing across the room as a fertility goddess, warm and wet and large, two tiny woodpecker chicks swaying from my breasts, one sitting atop my protruding stomach, and dozens more clinging to my swinging hips as I danced the Mother dance, a kind of sultry step of abandon. The arms swinging in exultation, eyes closed, loose skin flapping against my thighs in beat with my slightly open mouth. "Wah, a Wah, a Wah, Wah, Wah."

And Sam looked on, serene in the accomplishment of all these children, watching me dance and clapping to the beat of my flapping belly and thighs and breasts with a sound of his own. "Ooh," he purrs. "a Ooh, a Ooh, Ooh, Ooh."

And I pick up the Pompeii statuette and twirl her around with me, rubbing her against my body, saturating her with my sweat. And I throw her to Sam who catches her and caresses her until she begins to move, waking up from her long slumber. "Ah," she moans. "Ah, a Ah, a Ah, Ah, Ah." As she thrusts her pelvis forward, finally releasing the *two-thousand-year-old* baby.

And when I woke this morning, Pericles is nestled in my arms, feeding at my breast. But when I show Pericles to Sam, he gives me a strange look. So I run out to display Pericles to the other mothers. They're all on the street with their strollers, chatting about, "My child said 'dog' for the first time today." So I pipe in, "Well my Pericles said today, 'Mama, did you know that the sins of the fathers are not visited on their sons, but on the mothers who brag about their children?'" Then the mothers turn amongst themselves and say, "How could she possibly understand? She hasn't experienced the blood and mess and placenta of birth, the extreme pain that can only be born by the true mother." "But I have experienced pain," I say. "Pericles knows the pain I have born." So I come back to Sam, and complain that the other mothers won't pay attention to Pericles. But he starts to yell at me. "Stop it. Just stop it. There is no Pericles. There will never be a Pericles. Just face it. We are mutant beings." I hug Pericles tightly against my stomach, protecting him from Sam's words. And in this crouched position, I freeze.

SQUARE ONE by Steve Tesich

DIANNE and Adam, a couple in their thirties, meet in a dystopian country in the future where everyone lives "cooperatively" and all feelings, art, and individuality have been co-opted by the state. But Dianne is a loner whose every instinct is to fight for her individuality. Sometimes, this makes her appear to the others to be moody. As when she refuses to go to the movie—playing in their building—that everyone else is going to see:

SCENE: Their apartment—a rocking chair, stuffed animals.

TIME: The future.

DIANNE: I'm not going. *(She sits down.)* What's it called? You know, when they have music in a movie. [ADAM: Movie music.] There's a name. [ADAM: The score.] That's it. The score. I can't bear those movies where some poor guy doesn't know the score. You know. You see a movie and there's some...poor guy just sitting at home minding his own business, thinking his thoughts... [ADAM: Man sitting at home thinking his thoughts. Sounds like a blockbuster.] All right. He's at home with his wife or mistress or lover and they're giggling and exchanging pleasantries. He's planning a ski vacation to Switzerland. He's feeling wonderful. But all the time there's this music playing. There's this music that we can hear but that he can't. And this music is telling us that there's a man waiting in the garage ready to plunge a knife into his heart. The music tells us that the woman he's with, the one he thinks he's taking on his ski vacation, is in on the scheme. She knows about the man in the garage. She knows about the knife. She's in on the betrayal. Everyone's in on it except the poor guy in question because everyone can hear the music except for him. All he hears are the words being spoken. [ADAM: I know this movie. There's no knives. Nobody gets murdered. It's a love story.] I've seen one of those. This couple falls in love and then they go shopping. They go shopping while the music plays. What's that called when they run around in a movie and live life to the hilt while the music plays? [ADAM: A montage.] That's it. They're both in this montage where time passes and music plays. They have kids. One second, the kids are tiny. The next, they're old enough to go shopping by themselves. The next, they're leaving home to start a montage of their own. Moments of life appear. Disappear. Their lives fly by like Christmas cards. The montage machine is making mincemeat of them all but they don't mind. They're happy. They smile. Time passes. Music plays. It's worse than murder.

STARTING MONDAY by Anne Commire

A casual acquaintance between two women in their thirties, Lynne, an illustrator, and ELLIS, a would-be director grows into a fierce attachment even after Ellis has moved to Los Angeles. When Ellis contracts cancer, Lynne shepherds her friend through the stages of the illness that will eventually kill her. Not yet aware that she has cancer, she knows she's not feeling well. Until now she's been a dynamo of enthusiasm and hope.

SCENE: Ellis is in bed in her garishly painted L.A. house.

TIME: The present.

ELLIS crawls under L.A. quilt, grocery bag on floor, headphones on bedpost. Sun trying to peek through drawn shades. Writes in journal. Stops. Thinks aloud. Voice is a little less energetic.

ELLIS: I was sick again all weekend. There's a thousand things I should be doing, like working on this house. I thought I'd earn enough to fix it, but I got fired. Well, not fired. They didn't renew my contract. It felt like fired. It was fired. *(Beat)* I set out to prove I was a good director; all I proved was the need for perfection and two shows a week make you tired. And every month there'd be this pain. The crew'd have coffee breaks, I'd have vomit breaks. I didn't dare tell them. It's so hard for women to break into television, and cramps is such a lame excuse. Wednesday, I had spearmint tea, two Naprosyn, and an Alka Seltzer Plus. I'd like to call Lynne, but I don't dare. People get to know me, then walk away. Or did I walk away? *(Grabs stomach)* Maybe I'm just depressed about this hysterectomy business. I went to one of the best doctors in Beverly Hills five months ago. She said it was all in my head. Now, this doctor says fibroids. "My body and my brain are my servants not my master." *(Beat)* Thursday, I had three ounces of veal, four ounces of spinach, and a brief affair. Why does going to bed with someone you don't even care about hurt so much when they don't call after? I guess I feel he didn't respect me. I guess I didn't respect myself. I guess I don't trust men. *(Beat)* I'd like to call Lynne, but I don't dare. When you start to depend on someone, you give away too much power. Mom is so needy—I don't want to be like that. You can't depend on anyone, ever. It's as simple as that. *(Laughs)* I guess I don't trust women. *(Beat)* Starting Monday, I'm going to run five miles around the lake whether I have cramps or not; mail ten resumes instead of five; call eight people instead of four; go to Paramount, go to Warner's. Signed Ellis Crowley. I can't keep calling Lynne.

THE SWAN by Elizabeth Egloff

In this black comedy fantasy, a much-married woman, DORA, in her thirties, finds a swan in her Nebraska home. The swan has assumed the form of a man named "Bill." Dora becomes his protector, teacher and moral guide. Here, she explains to him about modern, human life—she's playing cassettes in a boom box.

SCENE: Dora's house.

TIME: The present.

DORA: Clothes, on the other hand, are very important. Duane, the first time I met Duane, he was wearing a French suit, Italian shoes, and a Brazilian crocodile coat. Duane had more clothes than anybody I ever met. Then he got a job on an oil rig, and asked me to marry him. I'll never forget the day I waved him off at the pier. I was wearing a red tulle dress, six-inch yellow heels, and a little white pillbox hat. I couldn't stop crying for a month. *(She stops, and looks at him.)* That looks much nicer. You need a tie. There. On the floor. You only get one chance to make a first impression. *(He hands her the tie. She takes it and starts to tie it around his neck.)*

You ever been married, Bill? I'm a great supporter of marriage. I don't think people are meant to be alone. I don't think I am. Strange things happen to me when I'm alone. Dangerous things. Like once I was in bed smoking a cigarette. And I'm lying there and I look up and I see a man standing in the door. He just walked into the house. He just opened the door and walked right into my house...And he's covered with leaves and there's grass in his hair and mud on his shoes. And he looks so sad and he looks so much like Gerry only that was before I'd ever met Gerry so how could he BUT there's something about him there's something in him that's warm that's comfortable someplace I could ease my aching heart and God: I looked at this person, I looked at this total stranger and I thought Yes you're right love is the only thing that matters if only I could get me some I could laugh again I could eat again I could belong to the world again, and just as I'm about to say Yes, you're him You're the one, my cigarette is burning my fingers and I turn to put it out, and by the time I look back, he's gone. Disappeared. Evanesced. I never saw him again. It's always the way, isn't it? Some people say I shouldn't marry so many, but I have to. They keep disappearing on me.

Franklin always said, he said, Dora if you can't love yourself, then you can't love anyone. I said, but Franklin...I love you...Franklin was much too delicate for someone of my affections. If he hadn't left, I probably would have destroyed him altogether.

I don't think men are born on this planet. I think men are born on the planet Pluto and they have them molecularly disassembled and radared to the earth. Which is why. Which is why they are so, so, you have to take care of them in a very special way because they are foreign bodies being introduced to the system. And which is both why I love them and why I don't understand them whatever they're talking about.

I remember I met Gerry, you would think it was the day after he'd been radared to the earth. There was something about Gerry. Something tender, something baby, like here was a man who needed more time to adapt to the eco-system. Gerry was always talking to himself: What is love and why do we do it? The day after we got married he went out in the woods and shot himself. The whole thing didn't exactly inspire my confidence.

Duane inspired my confidence, or what was left of it. Duane breathed life into a millimeter of myself, the piece of shrapnel I have come to regard as my heart. I took one look at Duane and said, here's a man he doesn't ask questions, and he doesn't own a gun. Perfect, I thought, how could I go wrong? So I told him I loved him, and I loved myself. Duane said, how can you love yourself, if you don't love the world? Love the world, I said? I can hardly get out of bed. *(Beat)* Two days later, he ran off. I was joking.

THE TALENTED TENTH by Richard Wesley

TANYA, a modern black woman of twenty-four, confronts Pam, a light-skinned black woman in her late thirties, whose husband is leaving her for Tanya. When Pam says her husband will prove too much for Tanya, Tanya replies.

SCENE: Tanya's apartment.

TIME: The present.

TANYA: My father is the owner of three bars and two barbecue restaurants. My mother is the principal of a grammar school down in Newark. I did my undergraduate studying at Spelman College and

114

graduate work at Columbia. I work for the largest newspaper in New Jersey. The silver spoon that was in my mouth when I was born was made by my grandfather on my mother's side who was the richest black preacher in North Carolina...at least that's what they tell me. I have always been used to having things...anything... anytime...anywhere...anyhow.

At Spelman, I belonged to that gathering of individuals loathed above all others on college campuses: a clique. Loathed mostly by people who never had any hope of joining. In my group were the daughters of doctors, lawyers, businessmen, and career military officers...We had money, you understand...we could *do* things. Women who can do things are most prized by men who can do nothing...the problem is, of course, that women like me want men who can do everything...Men who can do things want women who can do nothing, because such women provide no competition and are eternally grateful to these men for giving them station in life...Thus, here I am, attractive, successful, living in a penthouse overlooking everything; unmarried, childless, and alone...kept on an emotional string by a man who is married to one of those do-nothing women...All I have to do is tell him it's over...I should, really...but I've always been used to having whatever I've wanted...I want him...and I know that she can't keep him forever...This situation has taught me something I never thought it necessary to learn, being a black girl with a silver spoon in her mouth...patience. It's more than a virtue...it's a weapon.

All my life, I've had to deal with stuck-up yella bitches like you. Y'all think you're God's gift, with your sense of tradition and your money, and your mixed heritage and all that other shit. I've watched you all get by on nothing more than your looks. What blondes are to brunettes, you bitches are to us. Well, I got your man, honey. Little old black-as-night me and I'm gonna keep him. I don't care how much you know about him, or how many kids y'all got. I don't care if you win every penny in the divorce settlement. I'll still have *him*...and whatever he loses I'll build back up for him *double*. And that means twice as much money, twice as many kids *and* twice as much *woman*!

115

TALKING THINGS OVER WITH CHEKHOV by John Ford Noonan

Jeremy, early forties, has written a play about his past relationship with MARLENE, an actress in her thirties. He runs into her in the park and gives her the play. Marlene expresses admiration but insists that Jeremy rewrite the second act. During their next encounter, she persuades him to try.

SCENE: On and around a bench in Central Park, New York City.

TIME: The present.

MARLENE: The opening night audience. *(MARLENE "acts out.")* Curtain up. Me and the guy playing you charge out of the gate. No more than ten minutes and we've got them riveted. They gasp at the first act ending. The lobby's buzzing. Hear the buzz? Catch the chatter? *(Suddenly "imitating WOMAN" in lobby.)* "O GOD, IRENE. THE MALE CHARACTER'S JUST LIKE MY FRED!" Look over in the corner. Two gays giggling. *(Acts out "Two gays giggling.")* And that eighty-two-year-old blue-haired lady in mink whispering to the boy working the concession stand. *(Suddenly imitates "eighty-two-year-old lady.")* "...HAD I DIED LAST YEAR, I WOULD'VE MISSED THIS!" Your first act has unified the crowd. Now they're filing back in for the second act. They're expecting the birth of a true, honest-to-goodness original. They all want to be able to say, "YES, I WAS THERE THAT INCREDIBLE NIGHT." Jeremy, the second act as written now and they'll get angry. Mad. You promised roses and delivered dandelions. [JEREMY: Yesterday you said it was the greatest thing since—] And the critics! The one, clear, unmistakable thing that unifies them is disappointment. Once a year on Broadway they let their anger out, not at some amateur American or overrated Britisher, but at some promising talent who pumps them up in Act I and doesn't deliver in II. Please don't let them hang you by the ankles. Please don't let them make you never want to write again.

TASSIE SUFFERS by Ken Friedman

An actress in her twenties in a coffee shop tells her friend about her most recent audition.

SCENE: A coffee shop

TIME: The present

TASSIE: My day? You want to hear about my day? No, you don't! Does anyone really give a damn about my day? No! But, you asked! So, okay, I'll tell you. Today, I spent three and a half hours on line waiting for another goddamned audition. I know. I know...But, it was for this daring, new avant-garde theater group that was going to do *The Cherry Orchard* in a totally wild way: Outdoors in a real forest. Yes! and everyone gets to chop down a tree! Hey, I went. And there must have been over a hundred actors in line, several with sharpened axes. Why didn't I think of that? All I had on was a peasant apron, my red babushka, and heavy boots. But, I looked terrific. For what? Because, just as I'm nearing the head of the line; just when I'm up to my ass in emotional borscht; the word came out: THEY CHANGED THE PLAY! You heard me. Changed it! Four from the door and it was now an untitled comedy about a vegetable market in Trenton, New Jersey. Is that stupid? But, there were three roles for women. A ghetto teen: tough, but who secretly reads Plato; an aging produce woman who once had an affair with Fidel Castro (remember him?) and an oversexed librarian who loves young boys more than she loves old books. When I read that list, I flipped. I'm right for all of them! But, now I'm at the door and I'm still wearing my goddamn boots. I'm screwed! "Next!" I go in. "Okay, Tassie, do you know the roles that are open? Three women. Good. Honey, relax. Take a few moments...and improvise." "Huh? Improvise what?" "Improvise. We want to see what you can come up with. Be free. Have fun. Enjoy."

Have fun? Enjoy? You nitwit! Have you been standing in line since Tuesday? My throat is dry. My hands are wet. And who the hell am I supposed to be? The tomato-selling Cubaphile, the philosophic juvenile, or the oversexed pedophile? They waited. I waited. And then it happened. I exploded. I burst into the greatest single audition ever given anywhere by anyone! I was all three at once! A Cuban cashier telling an eight year old Plato to shut his goddamn mouth in the public library! And then I was a New Jersey dictator stealing fruit from an aging teenager who wanted more from life than papayas and apples! And more. And more! I went up, down, in and out and beyond in an incredible torrent of amazingly perfect choices. Weeping, dancing, loving, and walking as three people at once! Acting? Ha! Above acting. Fission, baby! Fission! I flared! I seared! I was fire.

And when it was all over I stood panting in a silence that deserves to be called: enchanted. I waited. My head bowed. And finally, one of them, a man who looked sort of worried, said: "Thank you...very...interesting..."

Interesting? Is the goddamn Venus DeMilo interesting?

"Thank you, uh...Miss Manson. Do you need your picture?..."

And so I left. Again. I walked out...But, I was great! They may not know it, because they measure me against themselves. But, I know what I did. And so do you. And as of today, I am special! No matter what they say! I mean, what the hell do those murderers know? So, of course, well now I am a little let down. A little depressed. But, I'll be fine. God. So, that was my day. Okay, now how the hell was yours?

THOSE THE RIVER KEEPS by David Rabe

Phil, an ex-con from Mulberry Street, has beaten up his wife Susie. She returns to the apartment with her friend, JANICE, in her thirties, a confidant since their waitressing days. In a monologue created for this book from dialogue in the original play, Janice is urging Susie to pack up and leave.

SCENE: An apartment in the Hollywood flats.

TIME: The present.

JANICE: Susie, this is what happens when you are locked up with no other human contact except a guy like Phil too long; your self-worth, your autonomy starts to rot. I have to say that more than once in this last segment, you seemed determined to take the art of masochistic bullshit to its limits and I didn't think I could bear to watch another second.

(*Giving SUSIE a little hug*)

I mean, you know those times when recently I didn't return your calls right away—I felt awful.

(*She heads for the cupboard to get wine glasses and pour the wine*)

But there were just hours of the night when I didn't think I had the necessary immunities. I would feel, for godsake, what if it's contagious, this self-deluded way of relating to your own needs and what are other peoples worst traits. Not that I haven't tried to exit the freeway by means of the On Ramp, myself. I mean, I know if you want to waste several years in a demented relationship, you have to pick the guy with great care. But upon occasion, it seemed you had outclassed the field. Can you imagine how macabre you must have appeared—for me to feel I had lost all points of personal reference?

I mean, where is Denise? Right? Where is she?

The three of us were so close. But where is she now? I liked Denise. I loved Denise.

But it wasn't real. I always knew it was never real.

(*She puts pizza in oven.*)

It was just the circumstances, we were all indentured to that same nitwit restaraunteur. But when those things changed, there was nothing to keep her with us.

(*As SUSIE returns from bedroom with a pile of clothes and a plastic bag of laundry. As she moves to the couch and starts to fold the clothing. Preparing to pack, JANICE moves to join her.*)

But you and me, we're still here, and do you know why? Because I think we have something permanantly in common.

You remember how mad you got at me that first time I told you how I honestly felt about Phil?

That was almost the end for us, if you remember.

It started on the phone, but it got quickly too heavy, so we met at that cute little bar with the whale motif.

[SUSIE: And drank twenty-seven cappuccinos apiece, because we didn't want to drink wine, the subject was too important to get soused.]

Right, so we ended up talking like a couple of amphetamine queens! Yabbidda, yabbidda.

No, no, no, no, no. That was the whole point. You WEREN'T

119

married—you were THINKING ABOUT getting married. You had met him and moved in with him, but—you were in that little apartment in West Hollywood, the one with the phony Mexican door and the sickening pea-green shag rug.

Right. And across the street was The Tart, Clarice.

With her vinyl pedal pushers and her ever-expanding thunder thighs. She was like the prototype for some form of advanced slut.

It was probably this constant display across your street that made Phil, by comparison, look human. So there you were talking about marrying this guy and the whole horrific scenario was like in electric color right before my eyes. I mean, if ever there was a Gumba who, they should not have let his antecedents off Ellis Island—it was him. But I could not get through to you. It was like some hidden adversary was jamming my signals.

Next thing I know, you're screeching at me that you wouldn't stand for me to judge you like that.

But I wasn't I kept trying to tell you. I wasn't judging you, I was judging him, I was warning you.

And then when you went into the baby madness—I mean, I wanted to ask you, do you feel no responsibility to the aesthetic requirements of the world? I mean, the Environmental Protection Agency will have your name on some official penalties list you start procreating with this set of chromosomes, they have a face like a cannoli, somebody took a bite out of it—they threw it away, somebody else stepped on it, he's what's left. How does anybody manage such a nose that takes so long to arrive at this idiotic point, and these eyes set in there like day-old rat turds in the snow. I did not know what to conclude except you had lost your mind because there WE WERE in the land of surferbodies, the land of the lean, the sun-tanned and the blonde, guys who are the result of a rigorous devotion to sun and oil and Nautilus, and there you were in this adolescent snit over this meatball from an unknown planet, he should not have left Mulberry Street ever.

I mean, you are not suggesting that you have taken offense because you feel I have defamed this bozo?

THREE BIRDS ALIGHTING ON A FIELD by Timberlake Wertenbaker

The vacuous pretensions of the art world are on display in this posh London art gallery. BIDDY, a woman in her thirties, married to a Greek tycoon and used to being ignored—the proverbial mouse—awakens to her own authentic sense of self. No one is more surprised than she that her opinion counts.

SCENE: London.

TIME: The present.

BIDDY: I didn't at first understand what was happening. For someone like me, who was used to being tolerated, it came as a surprise. You see, before, everything I said was passed over. Well, smiled at, but the conversation would continue elsewhere. I was like the final touches of a well decorated house. It gives pleasure, but you don't notice it. England still had women who went to good schools, and looked after large homes in the country, horses, dogs, children, that sort of thing, that was my voice. Tony—that's my first husband—said he found my conversation comforting background noise when he read the papers.

But then, silences began to greet everything I said. Heavy silences. I thought there was something wrong. Then I noticed they were waiting for more words, and these words had suddenly taken on a tremendous importance. But I was still saying the same things. You know, about shopping at Harrod's, and trains being slow, and good avocados being hard to come by, and cleaning ladies even harder. And then, I understood.

You see, I had become tremendously rich. Not myself, but my husband, my second husband. And when you're that rich, nothing you do is trivial. If I took an hour telling a group of people how I had looked for and not found a good pair of gardening gloves, if I went into every detail of the weeks I had spent on this search, the phone bills I had run up, the catalogues I had returned, they were absolutely riveted. Riveted.

Because it seemed everything I did, now that I was so tremendously wealthy because of my second husband, mattered.

Mattered tremendously. I hadn't expected this, because you see, my husband was foreign, Greek actually, and I found that not—well, not quite properly English you know, to be married to a Greek—after all, Biddy *Andreas?* I could imagine` my headmistress—we had a Greek girl at Benenden, we all turned down invitations to her island—and Yoyo—that's my husband, George, Giorgos, actually—he didn't even go to school here—but he was so rich and I became used to it—him, and me: being important.

VIOLENT PEACE by Lavonne Mueller

KIM's mother died when she was six months old. Kim's father is a General. Mark, her father's young adjutant, was given the job of supervising Kim's upbringing. In this scene, Kim is now twenty-one and in love with Mark. Kim tells Mark, forty-two, why she loves him and also why it's so difficult to grow up among warriors.

SCENE: A hotel room.

TIME: The present.

KIM: I learned everything about women from men's girlie magazines. And from mortar shells I looked at in the skies of Jalapa. *(A beat)* Some shells flirt and whimper…like little girls. Others crack bright and loud—like Mae West setting up for her lovers. Some shells explode like wild sperm leaking across the sky in silvering milk.

(A beat)

Did you ever think about how you sounded? I was a little girl playing by the kitchen table when you and Daddy were talking: Getting in…pulling out…holding on…taking the breast of a hill…squeezing off a shot…getting on top…pump the old M-16…forward thrust…blasting off…I grew up thinking women were the enemy. I was 20 before I found out love didn't look and smell like war.

(A beat)

Why do you think I tried to shave my hair off when I was three? So I could be bald. Like Daddy. Why do you think I wore brass on my snowsuit and made everybody salute me? So I could be like Daddy. (*A beat*) After a while, he faded out. And it was only you.

(*A beat*)

You taught me men had feelings. Yes. That's the truth. I grew up surrounded by soldiers...groveling, quaking around my father. I thought they just jumped when you asked them to. That's what they did for Daddy all the time. And that's what they did for me. Later on...when I was older...well, they still jumped. Sometimes they got erections, groaned, sighed a little, wiggled in a moment of pleasure, and then snapped back to attention. And then...when we made love for the first time...when I got back from Switzerland...on my 18th birthday—that night at the Officer's Club. You danced with me. And I knew then. I knew that night how much you wanted me. You were wearing tropical dress. Stiffly starched and dazzling white. The creases so sharp it was hard to lie down. Those little gray hairs over your ear were marked blue from your pen. You wanted to rub the blue off, but I wouldn't let go of your hand. I told you how the amazons in mythology defeated the enemy. They raised their skirts and showed their genitals. The other side ran in fright. You shook more. I drew a bead on you as you lay there. Powerless. I knew the rules. My training's along thin, light, quick-hitting lines. I must go deep. I made you cry.

(*A beat*)

I never knew a man felt pain.

WAY DEEP by Katherine Wilcox Burger

Two bright teenagers—JOLENE and Tate—fall in love and decide to run away. On the road, the first blush of love turns sour as they face the real world, and they decide to return home.

SCENE: Two ratty lawnchairs on a scruffy piece of lawn.

TIME: The present.

JOLENE is fifteen. She wears baggy black clothes and no make-up. She looks serene and otherworldly, a sixteenth-century madonna

123

(religious, not rock icon)

JOLENE: What I've heard is: there are only two stories in the whole world. "A stranger comes to town," and "I go on a journey." Everything else—boy gets, loses, recovers girl; X betrays Y over Z, Y stabs Z with a corkscrew—it's all variations on the theme. Someone you know can turn out to be a stranger, and the other way around. A journey can be local. Not everyone has the wherewithal to travel. And some journeys are inner, and I don't mean *The Incredible Voyage*, those medical rescue people bopping around in some guy's bloodstream. Sometimes a person is exposed to, I don't know, a new thought, a different perspective, and it's as boggling as if they'd gone to outer space.

So here's the deal. In the summer of my fifteenth year a stranger showed up in town and I ended up going on a journey and then I went home again. In a nutshell. But it was more complicated than that, at least to me. I guess I should start at the beginning. He—the stranger—was visiting his aunt Betsy because his parents were getting a divorce and they wanted him out of the way. The first time I saw him I felt like all the air in my chest just got compressed, as if a hand was squeezing my heart. It didn't get any better. It was, like, agony to see this guy. Not seeing him was worse; I'd moon around and wear black a lot, even though it was summer, and look in the mirror for skin imperfections for hours. It's embarrassing to admit how much time I spent looking in that mirror. Maybe I was trying to go through the looking glass and find a backwards world where I'd fit in more. And then one day he spoke to me.

I was nutzoid, gonzo, gone.

We started having these really deep conversations, not a lot of gossip and hot air like the other kids. We talked about important stuff. Big stuff. The eternal questions. Death, life on other galaxies, is there a god or is life just a panoply of chaotic happenstance.

I brought a blanket and some iced tea.

I know what you're thinking: teenagers, a blanket, the stars—but it wasn't like that.

But then he touched me.

He touched me and the world was never the same again. And all above us the stars were streaming, streaking through the black night sky with a dying fall, like music too lovely to be heard, too lovely to live.

I wanted to die. I figured that whatever else happened during the whole rest of my life it would never be as good as this. I wanted to die right now.

WHAT A MAN WEIGHS by Sherry Kramer

JOAN, thirty-five, works in the book restoring department of a university library. Things feel better to her when she can make them funny. She's just had a furious and passionate kissing session with a man she works with. Now he's expecting more.

SCENE: Joan's apartment.

TIME: Late at night.

JOAN: You know what the French say, don't you? The French say it is never as good as it is when you are first climbing the stairs. So...it *was* good. Really good. It was fabulous. Thank you. So—I once spent a week with a man named Charles at one of those useless bookbinder conventions—everybody sharing the recipe for the perfect non-binding glue, that sort of thing. It was spring, which in France means one thing, but in Nebraska, it means another. It means tornadoes. So, when the convention was over, our plane took off right into the middle of one. Half of all the really big guns in book conservation were on that plane, and I was imagining the headlines if it went down. LIBRARIANS PAY THE BIG FINE. And, PLANE OVERDUE. That sort of thing.

I was having an excellent time.

I knew that to die with that week I had spent with Charles inside me—to die, not full of fear, or longing, or regret, but full of that—that would be heaven.

I don't believe in heaven, do you? The French do, I suppose. But the airplane is an American invention. Which explains a lot of things.

Anyway, I didn't die—so much for my one shot at heaven—and, since staircases don't crash—we have to take responsibility ourselves. You said it is never as good as it is when you are first

125

climbing the stairs. I agree.

But the stairs didn't crash. We missed our chance.

That was as good as it was ever going to get. Why go on?

Can I get you something to drink? Juice? Water out of a bottle? Or something more...binding? Something that will bind itself to your red blood cells, make its way to your brain, and erase a few choice entries from those soft gray pages?

YANKEE WIVES by David Rimmer

MARCELINE DAVIS, a black woman in her early twenties, tries to maintain what she considers an actress's dignity, style, and grace. Quite often her funky, almost-catty, sometimes-ditzy side breaks through and takes over. Here, she has come up with an idea for marketing her husband, Billy D, and checks it out with the other Yankee wives.

SCENE: The Wives' Lounge for the Yankees—an old locker room redesigned for the ladies. This is where they spend their time before and after making their appearance at the games in support of their husbands. Over the years, they have become a sorority and regard themselves as a team.

TIME: Opening day of a recent season.

MARCELINE: Let me ask you something, okay? *(Takes a beat.)* How do you feel about candy as a career move? *(Crosses to the candy machine.)* Snickers, Three Musketeers, Milky Way, Almond Joy...the Billy "D" Bar. What do you think? Got a nice ring? I've been meetin' with these candy companies—Looks good—They seem up for it. I've always had this dream that someday Billy "D" Davis would be a candy bar. —It's just which kind—There's so damn many of 'em—Caramel, nougat, toffee, milk chocolate—*(MARCELINE smiles.)* Now's the time, darlin'—You know what I say—We only got a few years—Athletes die twice and all that. When you're hot you're hot, and when you're not you're nothin'. And we're hot now, and I'm takin' this bull by the horns, I'm puttin' all my energy into it, and I promise you, by the end of this year, I will make Billy "D" Davis a *major* candy bar!

YANKEE WIVES by David Rimmer

RONNIE, in her twenties, gung-ho, wild dresser, not the kind you'd call subdued, tells the wife of a rookie about ballplayers' habits.

SCENE: The Wives' Lounge for the Yankees—an old locker room redesigned for the ladies. This is where they spend their time before and after making their appearance at the games in support of their husbands. Over the years, they have become a sorority and regard themselves as a team.

TIME: Opening day of a recent season.

RONNIE: They get pretty fussy about their good luck stuff. Like Dave—? He always has to have the same breakfast on the days he pitches—Bacon and eggs, two over easy, two sunny side up, eight pieces of toast—two for each egg—pancakes, coffee, orange juice, cereal—Captain Crunch if it's an Eastern Division club, Cocoa Krispies if it's Western—and a hot fudge sundae for dessert. So one day I ran out of hot fudge, so I put Bosco on the sundae—I figured he wouldn't notice, he'd be so intense about the game and he never notices anything about anything he eats anyway. He takes one bite, screams, "This isn't hot fudge!", throws the sundae across the room, it hits the refrigerator, splatters all over the place, Bob the cat has a heart attack, she runs right through the screen door like a cartoon, and I have to drive Dave to Howard Johnson's so he can have his hot fudge sundae.

YANKEE WIVES by David Rimmer

PAM MONDAY, twenty-one, with an athlete's body, is married to Danny, a rookie pitcher on the team. She was an Olympic champion swimmer. She's dressed like it's the first day of parochial school: penny loafers, plaid skirt, white blouse, cardigan sweater.

Here she tells the wives about life with Danny and breaking the "unwritten law" among them. She has slept with one of their husbands— Billy D—who's married to Marceline.

SCENE: The Wives' Lounge for the Yankees—an old locker room redesigned for the ladies. This is where they spend their time before and after making their appearance at the games in support of their husbands. Over the years, they have become a sorority and regard themselves as a team.

TIME: Opening day of a recent season.

PAM: Well I did the Olympics and all these people were asking me to do all this TV stuff all the time—I couldn't say no—I did everything. I never knew where I was going—I had jet lag all the time—I fell asleep in cabs. I was in this plane and I started feeling really weird and closed in, like I was gonna explode if I didn't get off the plane? And I thought, I really thought—would it be better to stay or jump? Into the ocean? I mean, cause it wouldn't hurt when I hit the water cause I was such a good diver?...When I got there I hid behind one of those big luggage carts, and the people meeting me didn't see me, so I got on another plane and came home...I went to high school with Danny and I saw him at a Christmas party and we wanted to get married on New Year's Eve, but we couldn't cause I had this bathing suit thing in the Bahamas that I couldn't get out of, so we waited until Valentine's Day, and by then it was Spring Training. He didn't think he'd make the team, so he made up all these rules to keep his intensity—No sex—No talking—He had Study Hour every night where you couldn't talk cause he was going over all the charts and the scouting reports. I tried to tell him—Don't try so hard, you can be intense without going crazy. He breaks this glass he's holding and starts yelling—I'm undermining his concentration—I don't want him to make the team cause I'm afraid he might become a bigger star than me—Then when he does make the team it's only cause of me, cause the Yankees want the publicity!? What—? What does he—? Then when I try to talk to him he goes into the bathroom—He can't get emotional cause it drains his energy and he's got a game tomorrow! I— What can I...? I saw Billy "D" at that Barbecue they have for the whole team. Danny was talking to the guys and Billy just started talking to me. He had this voice—like he could take care of anything. He poured me some wine—I don't know where he got it, everybody else had beer. He was so polite—even when he asked me to, you know. His voice was so soft I could hardly hear him, I—It didn't seem like anything bad, it just—All I had to do was go and he'd take care of everything. I just—I don't know why I went—I didn't have to watch what I was gonna say all the time—I didn't have to make things up— "Nice double play—" "Good throw—" I—

At least Billy "D"'s as good as I am!—I'm sorry!, but...So I went. I know I shouldn't've gone, but—What would you have done?

ZARA SPOOK AND OTHER LURES by Joan-Ackerman Blount

EVELYN—in her twenties—decides to put a little excitement into her life and some distance between her and her overprotective boyfriend, Talmadge—by entering the Bass n' Gal Classic in New Mexico: a fishing contest. Evelyn catches a fish—using the lure known as Zara Spook—and accepts her trophy as rookie of the year.

SCENE: Podium at Bass n' Gal Classics awards ceremony.

TIME: The present.

EVELYN: *(Clasping trophy)* Am I thrilled. I feel like I'm all the way up on the high dive. Now I know how Sally Fields felt. Larry Bottroff has informed me that she definitely is a state record, possibly the second-largest bass ever recorded but we need to verify it with the department of fish and game. 27.9 inches in length, 25 inches in girth, 21 pounds 9.44 ounces. Egg laden sow black bass, between 13 and 15 years old. Old enough to be in high school, be a cheerleader. Talmadge, are you here? Rookie of the year. I am truly honored.

She died...about an hour ago. We kept her alive for a good length of time with that new product Catch and Release, helps keep a fish alive through a stressful situation. It's the same effect as drinking Gatorade. I recommend it. She is a real beauty. Most of you have seen her but if you haven't and you want to she's in the big walk-in cooler at the back of the cafeteria, up on the shelf over the juices. Just ask Olive, she'll show you where, or her husband Bennie. You can find him at maintenance. Or I'll show you. You can find me...in the stars. I always heard the Classic was the ultimate and now I know it's true.

129

I want to thank Ramona and Teale for their support. I'm sorry they can't be here now. They're both still in the hospital. Room 204 you can visit them. Right above the juices, just kidding. And Margery, I want to thank Margery for all her help, some of you have met her, she pitched in with the decorations. And I want to thank Talmadge for giving me that fishing pole for Mother's Day three years ago, just a week after we met. He gave me this fish bowl with green jello in it, green jello with little Pepperidge Farm cracker fish floating in it, suspended in the jello. It was just darling. And he gave me a box of scented tissues which was real sweet of him cause I was still wrought up over Mister B. I have this little dachsund, Mister B. I call him Mister B. for Mister Big cause he's so small. What happened was this pack of wild dogs got him and drug him up the mountain up one end and back down the other. He managed to get home but he was real depressed; all bloody and some of his ribs were broken; they'd punctured his lungs. I knew if I took him to the vet that would be the end of him; they put them in those cages, you know, and given his mental state I knew he wouldn't make it so I just held him all night. When their lungs are punctured the air comes right up under the skin. I could feel it. So, I just started to squish him. I squished him and squished him, you know like when you pop those mailer sheets? Well, he made it. The next day I took him to the vet and he said I'd done the right thing, squishing that air back down inside him. Seemed like all he wanted was to be in my arms. Egg laden sow bass. Kind of sad...Anyhow. This is my first trophy ever. I did get a trivet once for a door prize but it doesn't mean diddlysquat to me. So. I don't want this moment to end. I don't want to get down.

ZARA SPOOK AND OTHER LURES by Joan-Ackerman Blount

MARGERY, in her twenties, is visiting the site of the Bass n' Gal fishing contest—the city of Truth or Consequences, New Mexico, a state she has always wanted to see. She hitched a ride with a gun-toting husband of one of the contestants.

SCENE: A phonebooth in Truth or Consequences, New Mexico.

TIME: The present.

MARGERY: *(speaking into phone)* Lydia, I'm thinking of coming home. I don't know, I guess I used to be a lot braver. I've been in my motel room all day until now, I'm in this phone booth outside, Lydia, picture me out in the desert holding on to a phone booth, holding on. The view? It's terrifying. The sky, the desert, there's too much...space, it just goes on and on how do people adjust to this. Someone's waving over there. I woke up this morning in a cold sweat, a cold sweat. I *am* upset. There's this cow skull over my bed, not a Georgia O'Keefe cow skull a real live dead cow skull. I was reading *Bonfire of the Vanities*, I could feel it staring at me so I put it in the closet. Immediately, there was this disturbance in the room, like I'd tampered with some sacred spirit, I put it back up and the jawbone, Lydia, the jawbone broke off in my hands. There are forces down here bigger than you or I—what is that person doing—primitive, raw forces so natural they're unnatural. No, no galleries, no jewelry, just a vast amount of vastness, my stomach, how did the pioneers ever make it to California. I feel like such a failure. I haven't been into town I don't have a car, some psychopath with a beanie shooter let me off here last night. I *was* going to Santa Fe my travel agent talked me into coming down here; she had some healing experience at these hot springs the Indians used to go to bathe their wounds, I don't know. This is where the first atomic bomb ever exploded, Lydia, that's the kind of energy I'm talking about.

Play Sources and Acknowledgements

Amsterdam, Diana, © 1993. ONE NAKED WOMAN AND A FULLY CLOTHED MAN. New York: Samuel French, 1991.

Anderson, Jane, © 1993. DEFYING GRAVITY. C/o The Author's Agent, Martin Gage, The Gage Group, 9255 Sunset Boulevard, Suite 515, Los Angeles, Californian 90069.

Bernstein, Douglas and Markell, Denis, © 1992. GETTING TO KNOW JEWS.

Blount, Joan-Ackerman, © 1993. ZARA SPOOK AND OTHER LURES. C/o The Author's Agent, Mary Harden, Bret Adams, Ltd., 448 West 44th Street, New York, New York 10036

Bodi, Sari, © 1993. HIDE THE BRIDE and SOUVENIR OF POMPEII. C/o The Long Wharf Theatre, 222 Sargent Drive, New Haven, Connecticut 06511.

Bottrell, David and Jones, Jessie, © 1993. DEARLY DEPARTED. New York: Dramatists Play Service, 1992.

Brown, Michael Henry, © 1993. GENERATIONS OF THE DEAD IN THE ABYSS OF CONEY ISLAND MADNESS. C/o Broadway Publishing, 357 West 20 St. New York, NY 10011.

Burger, Katherine. WAY DEEP. Copyright © 1992. In OFF-OFF BROADWAY FESTIVAL PLAYS SIXTEENTH SERIES. New York: Samuel French, 1992.

Busch, Charles, © 1991. RED SCARE ON SUNSET. New York: Samuel French, 1991.

Butterfield, Catherine. JOINED AT THE HEAD. New York: Dramatists Play Service, 1993. Copyright © Catherine Butterfield, 1992. CAUTION: The reprinting of JOINED AT THE HEAD included in this volume is reprinted by permission of the author and Dramatists Play Service, Inc., 440 Park Avenue South, New York, N.Y. 10016. No stock or amateur production of the play may be given without stock obtaining in advance, the written permission of the Dramatists Play Service, Inc., and paying the requisite fee. Inquiries regarding all other rights should be addressed to Gilbert Parker, c/o

by permission of Grove Press, Inc.

Kramer, Sherry, © 1990. WHAT A MAN WEIGHS. New York: Broadway Play Publishing, 1992.

Lucas, Craig, © 1993. CREDO. C/o The author's agent, Peter Franklin, William Morris Agency, 1350 Avenue of the Americas, New York, New York, 10019.

MacDonald, Ann-Marie, © 1990. GOODNIGHT DESDEMONA (GOOD MORNING, JULIET). C/o The Author's Agent, Susan Schulman, Susan Schulman Literary Agency, 454 West 44th Street, New York, New York 10036.

Mack, Carol K. MAGENTA SHIFT. Copyright © 1993. C/o The Author's Representative, Robert A. Freedman Dramatic Agency, Inc., 1501 Broadway, Suite 2310, New York, New York 10036.

Mamet, David, © 1992. OLEANNA. New York: Vintage Books, 1993. Reprinted by permission of Random House, Inc.

Margulies, Donald, © 1989, 1990. THE LOMAN FAMILY PICNIC. New York: Dramatists Play Service , 1990.

McNally, Terrence. LIPS TOGETHER, TEETH APART. New York: New American Library, 1992. From LIPS TOGETHER, TEETH APART by Terrence McNally. Copyright © 1992 by Terrence McNally. Used by permission of New American Library, a division of Penguin Books USA Inc.

McPherson, Scott. MARVIN'S ROOM. New York: New American Library, 1992. From MARVIN'S ROOM by Scott McPherson, Inroduction by Larry Kramer. Copyright © 1992 by Scott McPherson. Used by permission of New American Library, a division of Penguin Books USA Inc.

Melfi, Leonard, © 1993. BELLEVUE OF THE WEST SIDE and LAST CALL FOREVER.

Miller, Susan. NASTY RUMORS AND FINAL REMARKS. Copyright © 1979.

Mueller, Lavonne, © 1992. COFFEE AFTER THE STORM and VIOLENT PEACE.

Munro, Rona. BOLD GIRLS. Copyright © 1991 Rona Munro. C/o The Author's Agent, Mr. Tom Erhart, Cassrotto Ramsey Ltd., 60-66 Wardour Street, London W1V 3HP.

Nelson, Richard, © 1989. SENSIBILITY AND SENSE. London :

Rosenfeld, Seth Zvi. SERVY-N-BERNICE 4EVER. Copyright © 1988, 1992. New York: Samuel French, 1992.

Sanders, Nathan Eldon, © 1992. A GATHERING OF NETTLES. C/o Author's Agent, Helen Merrill, 435 West 23rd Street, #1 A, New York, New York 10011.

Shanley, John Patrick, © 1991. THE BIG FUNK. In 13 BY SHANLEY. New York: Applause Theatre Book Publishers, 1992.

Shein, Kate, © 1993. NON-BRIDALED PASSION.

Sherman, James, © 1989, 1990, 1992. BEAU JEST. New York: Samuel French, 1992.

Simon, Neil. LOST IN YONKERS. New York: Random House, 1992. From LOST IN YONKERS by Neil Simon. Copyright © 1992 by Neil Simon. Reprinted by permission of Random House, Inc.

Sondheim, Stephen; Weidman, John. ASSASSINS. New York: Theatre Communications Group, 1991. Text © 1990 and 1991 John Weidman, lyrics © 1990 and 1991 Rilting Music, Inc.

Swados, Elizabeth © 1992. GROUNDHOG. C/o The Author's Representative, Rosalind Lichter, Chasen and Lichter, Attorneys at Law, 1740 Broadway, New York, New York 10019.

Tesich, Steve. SQUARE ONE. New York: Applause Theatre Book Publishers, 1990. © 1990 Applause Theatre Books.

Tolan, Kathleen, © 1992. APPROXIMATING MOTHER. New York: Dramatists Play Service, 1992.

Wertenbaker, Timberlake © 1992. THREE BIRDS ALIGHTING ON A FIELD. London: Faber and Faber Limited, 1992.

Wesley, Richard, © 1989. THE TALENTED TENTH. C/o The Author's Agent, Mary Meagher, The Gersh Agency, 103 West 42nd Street, New York, New York 10036.

Whitacre, Bruce E, © 1993. A GENTILE OF THE TOP PERCENTILE. C/o Bruce E. Whitacre, The Manhattan Theatre Club, 453 West 16th Street, New York, New York 10011.

Wilson, Lanford. THE MOONSHOT TAPE. New York: Dramatists Play Service, 1990. © Copyright, 1990 by Lanford Wilson. CAUTION: Professionals and amateurs are hereby warned that THE MOONSHOT TAPE is subject to a royalty. They are fully protected under the copyright laws of the United States of America, and of all countries covered by the International Copyright Union (including the

Yankowitz, Susan. NIGHT SKY. New York: Samuel French, 1992.

Special thanks to David Cleaver and the entire staff of Applause Theatre Books for helping to assemble these monologues.

SOLILOQUY!

The Shakespeare Monologues
Edited by Michael Earley and Philippa Keil

At last, over 175 of Shakespeare's finest and most performable monologues taken from all 37 plays are here in two easy-to-use volumes (MEN and WOMEN). Selections travel the entire spectrum of the great dramatist's vision, from comedies and romances to tragedies, pathos and histories.

"Soliloquy is an excellent and comprehensive collection of Shakespeare's speeches. Not only are the monologues wide-ranging and varied, but they are superbly annotated. Each volume is prefaced by an informative and reassuring introduction, which explains the signals and signposts by which Shakespeare helps an actor on his journey through the text. It includes a very good explanation of blank verse, with excellent examples of irregularities which are specifically related to character and acting intentions. These two books are a must for any actor in search of a 'classical' audition piece."

ELIZABETH SMITH
Head of Voice & Speech
The Juilliard School

paper•MEN: Isbn 0-936839-78-3 • WOMEN: Isbn 0936839-79-1

APPLAUSE

A PERFORMER PREPARES

A Guide to Song Preparation for Actors, Singers, and Dancers

By David Craig

"David Craig knows more about singing in the musical theatre than anyone in this country—which probably means the world. Time and time again his advice and training have resulted in actors moving from non-musical theatre into musicals with ease and expertise."

—**Harold Prince**

"Studying with David Craig means infinitely more than learning how to perform a song. I find myself drawing upon this unique man's totally original techniques in all the arenas of my work. If mediocrity ever enters his studio, it is never allowed to depart."

—**Lee Remick**

"For those of us who were still terrified of singing, David Craig's class was the Second Coming... He is a master at creating exercises and tasks that release that talent, tasks that are measurable."

—**Lee Grant**

A Performer Prepares is a class act magically transformed to the printed page. It's a thirteen-part master-class on how to perform, on any stage from bleak rehearsal room to the Palace Theater. The class will cover the basic Broadway song numbers, from Show Ballad to Showstopper. With precise, logical steps and dynamic and entertaining dialogues between himself and his students, Craig takes anyone with the desire to shine from an audition to final curtain call, recreating the magic of his New York and L.A. coaching sessions.

CLOTH: $21.95 • ISBN: 1-55783-133-5

👏 APPLAUSE 👏

SHAKESCENES: SHAKESPEARE FOR TWO

The Shakespeare Scenebook

EDITED AND WITH AN INTRODUCTION BY JOHN RUSSELL BROWN

Thirty-five scenes are presented in newly edited texts, with notes which clarify meanings, topical references, puns, ambiguities, etc. Each scene has been chosen for its independent life requiring only the simplest of stage properties and the barest of spaces. A brief description of characters and situation prefaces each scene and is followed by a commentary which discusses its major acting challenges and opportunities.

paper ∎ ISBN 1-55783-049-5

MONOLOGUE WORKSHOP
From Search to Discovery
in Audition and Performance
by Jack Poggi

To those for whom the monologue has always been synonymous with terror, *The Monologue Workshop* will prove an indispensable ally. Jack Poggi's new book answers the long-felt need among actors for top-notch guidance in finding, rehearsing and performing monologues. For those who find themselves groping for speech just hours before their "big break," this book is their guide to salvation.

The Monologue Workshop supplies the tools to discover new pieces before they become over-familiar, excavate older material that has been neglected, and adapt material from non-dramatic sources (novels, short stories, letters, diaries, autobiographies, even newspaper columns). There are also chapters on writing original monologues and creating solo performances in the style of Lily Tomlin and Eric Bogosian.

Besides the wealth of practical advice he offers, Poggi transforms the monologue experience from a terrifying ordeal into an exhilarating opportunity. Jack Poggi, as many working actors will attest, is the actor's partner in a process they had always thought was without one.

paper•ISBN 1-55783-031-2

Michael Caine • John Cleese
Eric Bentley • John Houseman
Michael Chekhov • John Patrick Shanley
Cicely Berry • John Russell Brown
Jerry Sterner • Steve Tesich
Harold Clurman • Sonia Moore
Bruce Joel Rubin • Jonathan Miller
Josef Svoboda • Terry Jones
Stephen Sondheim • Larry Gelbart

These Applause authors have their work available
in discerning bookshops across the globe.

If you're having trouble tracking down an Applause title in your area, we'll ship it to you direct!

U.S. Customers: Include the price of the
book, $2.95 for the first book and $1.90 thereafter to cover shipping
(NY and TN residents:
include sales tax).
Check/Mastercard/Visa/Amex

Send your orders to: **Applause Direct**
211 West 71st St
New York, NY 10023
212-595-4735
Fax: 212-721-2856

U.K. Customers: Include £1.25 p&p for first title and 25p for each additional title.
Cheque/Master/Visa

Send your order to: **Applause Direct**
406 Vale Road
Tonbridge KENT
TN9 1XR
0732-357755
Fax: 0732-770219

Write or call for our free catalog of cinema and theatre titles.